# POWER FROM THE PEOPLE

# POWER FROM THE PEOPLE

Innovation, user participation, and
forest energy development

MATTHEW S. GAMSER

IT PUBLICATIONS 1988

Intermediate Technology Publications Ltd.
103/105 Southampton Row, London WC1B 4HH, UK

© Intermediate Technology Publications 1988

ISBN 0 946688 94 X

Printed in Great Britain by Short Run Press Ltd., Exeter

# Contents

# Figures and Tables

*DEFINITIONS*

LS = Sudanese Pounds
LS 1.30–3.30 = $ 1.00 (official value, 1982–1985)
LS 1.80–5.00 = $ 1.00 (parallel market value, 1982–1985)
1 FEDDAN = 0.42 HECTARES (approximately 1 acre)

# Acknowledgements

Many people have provided help and inspiration for this work. The staff of the Sudan Energy Research Council and the Sudan Renewable Energy Research Institute provided much advice, support and intellectual stimulation during my three years in Sudan. The US Agency for International Development (USAID) and the Government of Sudan provided essential funds for the technology development work that inspired this book. Energy/Development International and the Georgia Tech Research Institute, contracted by USAID to assist in the implementation of the Sudan Renewable Energy Project, provided the author with the Energy Economist position in SREP which enabled much of the research for this book to be undertaken. Other research, particularly that into user involvement in industrial innovation, was greatly assisted by the author's former colleagues from Sussex University's Science Policy Research Unit (SPRU) and by the library staff from both SPRU and the Institute of Development Studies.

A few key individuals deserve further mention: Andrew Barnett and Norman Clark of SPRU provided valuable critical advice and comment on this work. Dr. El Tayeb Idris Eisa, the Director of the Energy Research Council, and Donald B Peterson, Chief of Party for SREP, have given both friendship and instruction as colleagues during the author's years in Sudan. Neal Burton of IT Publications and Martin Elliot provided valuable editorial suggestions and other assistance. Finally special thanks are due to Anka Zaremba, for the editing and proofreading of earlier drafts, and for her general inspiration and support during the writing of this book.

# CHAPTER ONE
# Introduction

This book is a discussion of the management of technical change. It looks at many examples of this change, ranging from work on the most sophisticated, 'high-tech' products and processes for industrial cultures, to aspects of basic struggles for survival in rural areas in developing nations. Its heart lies in the detailed analysis of the introduction of forest energy technologies in Sudan.

The technologies themselves are not the focus of this study. Its central concern is the players who participate in their innovation, and the manner in which that participation can be organized. How technologies, in practice, affect the production or consumption of energy is important; but the ways in which institutions seek to generate these technologies, is of higher priority. Good change management, it will be seen, provides for the fullest use of local change resources. These resources consist of many types of knowledge and skills. They are obtained not only from formally trained scientists and technicians, who work within research and development facilities, but also from farmers, craftsmen, housewives, traders, and others outside the research and development (R & D) system. The latter group, while they may have little technical accreditation, have enormous technical change capability, gained from their experience in production, distribution, and consumption – the various dimensions of the use of technologies.

In some cases R & D work virtually by itself, carried out within laboratories and test stations, can bring about innovation. On the other hand, much technical change also occurs outside such formal R & D, as, for example, when the two young founders of Apple Computer spawned a new era of personal computing through tinkering in their garage. In most instances, several types of knowledge and skill contribute to the change process. The more location-specific the demands (physical and economic) on a technology, the more important is the role of technology user contributions in technical change.

Forest energy technologies are especially dependent on local social and environmental conditions. User participation in forest energy technology development is essential to innovation in this technology area. Promoting an approach that facilitates user participation in this process, therefore, is integral to change management, and to development assistance in this field. This work provides an empirical illustration of user importance through the analysis of forest energy technology development in Sudan.

1

'The historic and irreversible change in the way of doing things we call "innovation",' wrote Joseph Schumpeter in 1935, and this is the 'innovation' to be examined herein.[1] It is distinct from 'invention', which is the discovery of technical possibility. Innovation represents the marriage of this discovery with a specific application or applications. It contains both discovery and the satisfaction of a demand through that discovery. Until an invention finds a specific application in the form of a product or process, there is no innovation.[2]

Innovation is increasingly appreciated, as Rothwell and Gardiner describe it, as 'an iterative design process.[3] They and others have emphasized the important role played by 'technology users' in this design process. 'User' is a potentially ambiguous label, which in its narrowest sense can be held to indicate only those who 'use up', or consume a product, while in its widest interpretation can cover all persons who, through any means, interact with a technology, its creators, disseminators, and consumers.[4]

This book employs a broad definition of 'user', but not its most universal connotation. The 'users' it discusses fall into three general types:

1) Those who obtain a technology, through purchase or other means, in order to fulfill certain individual requirements. Examples of this type include housewives buying charcoal stoves to use in home cooking, farmers planting trees to provide fuel, poles, shelter, or other benefits for their land, or factory owners choosing a certain machine or process technique for their operation.
2) Those who mass-produce a technology, or who carry out production operations with its techniques. These users include artisans who manufacture stoves, assembly line staff who operate and maintain machinery, charcoal makers, and nursery builders and operators.
3) Those who disseminate, or distribute a technology to other users. This last group includes traders (wholesale and retail), marketing personnel, and teachers. It also contains extension agents and development assistance workers.

The user types may be referred to in shorthand fashion as 'consumers', 'producers', and 'distributors'. The three types are not mutually exclusive. This overall user domain does not contain the staff of universities, research laboratories, or other formally established R & D facilities, except for cases in which these individuals, in their spare time and outside their work duties, consume, produce, or distribute technologies. By such a definition R & D work stands as separate from technology use, and R & D environments are isolated from users. This definition is used not to reinforce this stereotype, but to show the negative consequences of such isolation for innovation.

The notion of 'participation', too, has been given many meanings in development literature. Cohen and Uphoff have attempted to systematize the various forms of participation that can occur, which represents a valuable step towards a greater understanding of local participation in

2

technology development efforts.[5] In their classification, participation takes place in four aspects of assistance programmes: decision-making, implementation, benefits, and evaluation. The analysis of the development of new products and processes and, in particular, the detailed observation of forest energy development in Sudan, focuses on the presence and importance of participation in all these areas, placing particular emphasis on user participation in decision-making and evaluation (including re-design) of technologies.

The central thesis of this book is that an *ex ante* commitment to greater user participation in technology development enhances the innovative propensity of a given firm or agency. Making use of this human resource, this 'people power', is an integral part of effective change management. This premise is supported by brief examples of innovations in Western industry and by a more thorough analysis of development assistance projects – with particular attention given to work in Sudan on three forest energy technologies – charcoal kilns, improved charcoal stoves, and agroforestry. The Sudanese example describes the user-involved technology development programme implemented by the Sudan Energy Research Council through the Government of Sudan and US Agency for International Development-supported Sudan Renewable Energy Project.

A corollary to this thesis is that the principles and benefits of effective change management are universal. User participation is as important to the design and development of computer software and Boeing 747s as it is to that of charcoal stoves and other technologies for the poor people of developing nations. There is no difference between so-called 'high' and 'low' technology in this respect. Users are not involved in all successful innovations, but they play a major role in cases spanning a vast number of nations and technical disciplines. Managers from both industry and development assistance need to acknowledge and utilize this people-powered change resource.

Development assistance, in particular, can learn some lessons from those developed country firms which have begun to reorganize the structure and approach of their research and development bodies, in order to increase user interaction in product design and development. Rather than replicating institutional hierarchies and management structures now being overhauled and radically altered in developed country firms, universities, and other research centres, support for technical change in developing nations should seek to emulate this new, more user-interactive approach. This book, in juxtaposing innovation experiences from both developed and developing nations, demonstrates not only why user participation is essential in both spheres, but also how user-orientated management techniques can find immediate and productive application in developing country institutions and assistance programmes. The Sudan Renewable Energy Project (SREP) was designed as an exploration in new technology development strategies. In particular, the project staff were instructed to give priority to

3

the 'commercialization' of SREP's forest energy technologies, by which USAID meant supporting their self-sustaining production and distribution. SREP's objective was not merely to show that technologies worked, but to produce innovations and changes to production and consumption patterns caused by the widespread introduction of these technologies. The staff were told to look for ways in which the existing productive sector of the economy could be involved in the project. They were warned against devoting undue time and effort to in-house research, and were advised to concentrate on taking 'viable' technologies out into field trial and application as soon as possible.

USAID and the Government of Sudan used their financial support for SREP to move technology development work out of the ERC's internal facilities into the user community. While less than $250,000 was provided for internal procurement activities, over $2.8 million was made available for renewable energy development grant (REDG) disbursements. The agreement between the two governments that established SREP stipulated that these REDG funds had to be allocated to individuals or organizations outside the ERC and its constituent bodies. In order to utilize the bulk of the finance offered for forest energy development under SREP, the ERC had to identify external parties who could contribute to innovation, and to encourage them, through the incentives offered by the grant resources, into initiating forest energy technology activities. The financial structure of SREP thus served as a powerful incentive for the ERC to develop links with technology users in its R & D programme.

The establishment of the grants mechanism as the centre of SREP activity meant that, even before decisions had been taken as to which technologies should be the object of SREP attention, the necessity for user participation in their development was acknowledged. SREP was established from the outset as an exercise in the interaction between an R & D institution and technology users.

The author's work with SREP began in October 1982, the project's commencement, and ended in October 1985, the completion of his contracted assignment in Sudan. Although the ERC's work under SREP was not completed by that time, the results of its first three years' effort led both USAID and the Government of Sudan to declare the project a success. The analysis of events in the development of charcoal production, improved charcoal stoves, and forestry technologies under SREP looks at the elements of this success, and shows the importance of user contributions to the innovations that were achieved.

This book consists of two parts. The first part examines developments in the theoretical understanding of the innovation process and the role of users within that process. It also reviews the reassessment of research and development strategy that has been undertaken in many development fields, and is now beginning in the renewable energy field. This reassessment demonstrates that much common ground exists between technical

4

change in industrialized, and in the developing nations. The second part looks in detail at the experience of a user-oriented technology development effort in the forest energy work of the ERC under SREP. The results obtained in this effort substantiate the importance of the user role in innovation established in the previous section.

Chapter 2 looks at users and innovation in both industrial and development contexts.

Chapter 3 discusses problems that have beset project implementation in the renewable energy technology area, focusing on work in forest energy, and on the relative isolation from user involvement of technology development work in this field. Chapters 4 to 7 contain the detailed study of forest energy development in Sudan, with one chapter on each of the three technologies examined, and an introductory chapter concerning energy and institutions in that nation. Chapter 8 discusses how technology development strategy, R & D institutional management, and development assistance programmes can be restructured to better attract and utilize user contributions.

# Innovation, Technical Change, and Development: the Importance of 'Users'

Herrera, in a perceptive essay on innovation in rural areas of developing nations, writes

> The basic principles involved in the generation of technologies for rural areas are also valid for the whole society, although the mechanisms for their implementation could be somewhat different. . . . Two of the essential elements [of rural innovation] . . . are the utilization of local knowledge, and the participation of the local people in the whole process.[1]

This chapter, in essence, is an elaboration upon Herrara's brief, but incisive points.

It has long been recognized that innovation is a fundamental determinant of economic development. Adam Smith saw 'the invention of a great number of machines which facilitate and abridge labour, and enable one man to do the work of many'[2] and their application in industry as a key force behind the increased productivity of his time. Marx and Engels regarded innovation as a central pillar of the capitalist system, noting 'the bourgeoisie cannot exist without constantly revolutionizing the means of production.'[3]

Understanding the factors that affect innovation, the influences that encourage and direct it, is a central goal of science policy studies. Rather than treating technical change as a 'black box' phenomenon, something that exists outside the causes and effects of economic systems, while itself influencing the progress and direction of activities within those systems, such studies place innovation as a part of the economic environment, subject to and, most important, controllable through the forces that govern this environment.[4] While there has been disagreement concerning which factors are the most significant for the initiation and maintenance of innovative activity, there remains the central conviction that innovation can be comprehended in economic terms, and can be managed through the formulation and implementation of incentives which stimulate technical initiative.

*The sources of innovation: the 'push-pull' debate*
As Christopher Freeman has noted, innovation is essentially a two-sided activity:

> On the one hand, it involves the recognition of a need or more precisely, in economic terms, a potential market for a new product or process. On

6

the other hand, it involves technical knowledge, which may be generally available, but may also often include new scientific and technological information, the result of original research activity.[5]

Much of the innovation literature of the past 30 years has been occupied with the question of which of these two facets is of greater importance. Scientists and engineers have tended to emphasize the role of original research, and to ignore or dismiss the contribution of market forces. Economists often have taken the opposite approach, portraying innovative scientific activity as responsive to market influences. Langrish and his associates categorized these two schools of thought as 'discovery-push' and 'need-pull' theories of innovation.[6]

The 'push-pull' debate has been a double-edged sword for the development of a greater understanding of the process of innovation. It has been a liability in that much of its arguments have centred upon a confusion of experience and terminology, and its methods governed by a desire to reduce technical change into a mechanistic, linear framework. It has been an asset in that it has generated enthusiasm for the detailed analysis of individual experiences of innovation within industries and within firms, which has led to an appreciation of the interactive design process that underlies much successful innovation.

In the diverse realm of industrial activity in Western nations it has not been difficult to find cases that support both discovery-push (also called science-push) and need-pull (also called demand-pull) as the dominant forces governing innovation. For example, devices such as the hovercraft began without any notion of what their specific applications could be in existing market situations.[7] Yet, most medical instruments have been developed specifically to satisfy existing needs, often by laboratory technicians themselves.[8] When analysts attempt to generalize from their sector studies to draw inferences about the relative importance of 'push' and 'pull' factors over the larger realm of innovation, they inevitably end up comparing apples to oranges, with suitably ambiguous results.

As Mowery and Rosenberg have pointed out in a detailed critique of several innovation case studies, the debate also has been confused by an inconsistent and, at times, inappropriate use of the term 'demand'. They note that, rather than demonstrating that innovation is introduced because the market demand for a specific product has increased, indicating a positive shift of the demand curve, many of the studies show that technological improvements allow a product to be sold at a lower price. This is not a demand shift, but a movement along the supply curve (see Figure 2.1, below.[9]

'Need' is often confused with 'demand' in these studies.[10] This, too, can be very misleading, for while a person may 'need' many things, he may only be able to afford a small number of them. A new product's or

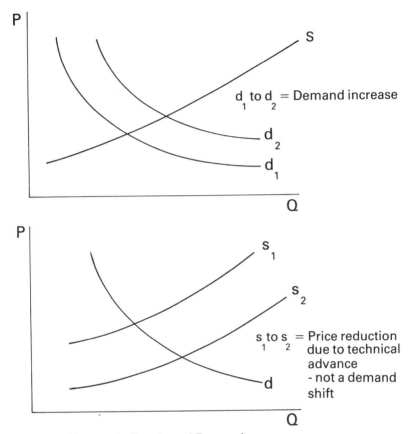

Figure 2.1 Changes in Supply and Demand

process's potential to satisfy existing needs is an important component of its success as an innovation, but it does not denote the primacy of demand factors in stimulating that innovation in the first place. Nor, because need cannot be equated with demand, can need satisfaction alone guarantee the market success of an innovation. If the product or process fulfils physical requirements, or needs, but is not affordable, it will not find enough applications to generate sustained technical change. Need and demand both are important factors in innovation, but their nature and their roles are not identical, and the 'push-pull' debate has hindered progress towards a better understanding of innovation in its blurring of the distinction between the two.

About the best that can be said about 'science-push' and 'demand-pull' factors is that both are potential influences on innovation, and that their individual importance will depend on the individual organization and product environment. Given the diversity of experience for individual

8

innovations, it seems pointless to attempt to find a single innovation prime-mover. Rather, investigators of industrial progress should acknowledge and attempt to understand a system of multiple forces, options, checks, and balances – and to admit the critical importance of innovation itself. As Freeman points out,

> Any firm operates within a spectrum of technological and market possibilities arising from the growth of world science and the world market. These developments are largely independent of the individual firm and would mostly continue even if it ceased to exist. To survive and develop it must take into account these limitations and historical circumstances. To this extent its innovative activity is not free or arbitrary, but historically circumscribed. Its survival and growth depend upon its capacity to adapt to this rapidly changing external environment and to change it.[11]

Freeman's quotation, while indicating the futility of attempting to characterize innovation as dominated by either technical or demand factors, also exposes the essence of more constructive developments that emerged from the empirical attention paid to technical change during the past three decades. These works, whether or not they foundered upon the difficulties of inter-sectoral comparisons or the isolation of market demand from supply factors, emphasize that innovation is a part of a larger environment populated by numerous influences, inclinations, and, of particular importance for this dissertation, abilities. The resources for innovation do not all lie within laboratories or within the R & D system, but also can be found in the firm's larger internal and external environment, in its own production and marketing systems, and in its relations to its suppliers, distributors, and customers. All those who use a technology, whether in production, trade, or consumption, possess a knowledge of it that can itself play a role in innovation. Case studies of innovations have helped to elucidate how such external knowledge has contributed to technical change, and how a firm's ability to identify and utilize this knowledge enhances its potential to sustain its innovative activity in its field.

## The Role of Technology Users in the Innovation Process

The recent empirical analyses of new product and process development have not been the first to point to technology user activity in innovation. Adam Smith, in 1776, noted

> A great part of the machines made use of in those manufactures in which labour is most subdivided, were originally the inventions of common workmen, who, being each of them employed in some very simple operation, naturally turned their thoughts towards finding out easier and readier methods of performing it.[12]

9

The newer work, however, lends valuable insight into the mechanisms by which inputs from outside the R & D system can be received and employed in both generating innovations, and in improving on the design and performance of existing designs and techniques. It does not show that users innovate or provide key ideas in all technology or industrial areas, but it does demonstrate that, in those areas in which user contributions are significant, a firm's capacity to channel these into its own R & D effort is an important determinant of its ability to remain innovative and competitive.

*Users as innovators*
Perhaps the most profound examples of user contributions to innovation are those cases in which the original conception and prototype version of the new product or process came from a technology consumer. This direct innovation by users is not all-pervasive. One does not and would not expect to find new petrochemical or pharmaceutical products generated outside R & D facilities. Yet, user innovation is not an influence only in 'low-tech' fields, such as food products and fashion design, but also in more advanced technological domains, such as scientific instrument production and software development.

Much of the pioneering work on user innovation has come from the Massachusetts Institute of Technology's Sloan School of Management and, in particular, from the research of Eric von Hippel and his students. Von Hippel's early work in this area studied the development of new products and processes in several fields, finding that 'in some industries, most commercially successful products are developed by product users, not product manufacturers.'[13] Virtually all successful new devices in the fields of scientific instrument production and semi-conductor electronics and sub-assembly manufacture initially were developed by people who had heretofore been customers for products from these industrial sectors. Moreover, a majority of the major functional improvements to established products in these fields were developed by customers. On the other hand, no new products in the polymer and plastics additives industries came from outside sources. In these sectors, manufacturer R & D-based innovation accounted for all new developments.[14]

As von Hippel continued to study user innovation he found that he was not the only person who appreciated customer contributions to technical change. Certain companies had created their own programmes to identify and encourage user innovation, and then to incorporate the most promising new products and processes into their own lines. IBM, for example, formed an Installed User Program department to attract and acquire user-developed programs for its medium and large computers. The company estimated that one-third of all its leased software originated from such user innovations.[15]

In a quite different field, the Pillsbury company initiated its annual Bake-Off in 1949 to publicize its flour and other bakery products. The company soon found that many of the recipes it received in this contest could be successfully marketed under the Pillsbury brand. One of its four cake mix lines and several variations of another stemmed directly from the recipes submitted by Bake-Off winners.[16]

But customers were not the only type of technology users who contributed important innovations in industrial fields. Marketing and distribution staff have come up with some of the most successful new product ideas of this century. Two of the most successful products of the Minnesota Mining and Manufacturing Company (3M), masking tape and Scotch tape, arose from salemen's initiatives. Peters and Waterman, in their analysis of the roots of 3M's success, saw the company's encouragement for all staff, not just its scientists and technicians, to contribute new product ideas, as the fundamental component of its ability to remain innovative.[17]

*User-R & D interaction in innovation*
Technology users do not have to supply the initial creative input to an innovation in order to play an important part in its success. Detailed analyses of new product and process development have pointed out that much technical change takes the form of incremental modifications to initial design ideas, and that some of the most successful ventures have a long history of critical reassessment and modification in response to user experiences with and requirements for the technology.[18] The interaction between users and R & D staff provides the impetus for this incremental innovation, which refines and strengthens the technologies brought forward in an initial creative impulse. Paul Gardiner and Roy Rothwell of the Science Policy Research Unit argue,

> What has not been highlighted, and should be, is that the tougher and more demanding the customers are in their requirements, the better and more robust the designs will be, along with their probability of reinnovation and propensity for successful longterm commercial exploitation.[19]

The two authors' study of innovations in the aeronautics and farm equipment sectors illustrates the positive results of this 'tough-customer' interaction. The development of the original Boeing 747 was a difficult and, at times, contentious process, as the manufacturer struggled to cope with stringent and fast changing requirements from Pan American Airways, its principal customer. Design specifications had to be continually upgraded. Moreover, Boeing had to build in a certain amount of 'stretch' into its initial design, as Pan Am raised new functional requirements, such as cargo carrying, that it might wish to see included in subsequent equipment orders. As a result, the 747 design that resulted was able to serve a wide variety of airline technical needs, and became a great success both for the manufacturer and its users.

R & D-user interaction need not occur or be confined to the formation of first commercial designs. User observations on established product characteristics and performance can be channelled into improved designs or the formulation of product off-shoots. The Howard Company's rotary cultivator, another Gardiner and Rothwell case study, did not experience extensive manufacturer-user interaction in its initial design. However, the company made extensive modifications and improvements to its design from its inception in 1962 to the present day, modifications heavily influenced by farmer comments and demands. Howard Company even operated a suggestion scheme to solicit farmer ideas. The authors comment,

> With the Howard Rotavator, the customer played a more 'reactive' role in the establishment of the original design specification, but subsequently adopted a more active (design-oriented) role in suggesting areas of improvement; it was a case of multiple interaction and producer/user complementarity.[20]

These two cases demonstrate only one type of user role, that of the customer, in design and innovation, but this role can and has been taken up by other types of technology users. The development of hovercraft, also analyzed by Rothwell and Gardiner, provides an excellent example of the various types of users and user contributions that can be involved in the innovation process. Hovercraft began as a technical conception with no specific end-use in the mind of its inventor, Christopher Cockerell. It had potential marine, aeronautical, and military applications, and, between the time of Cockerell's first patent and the commercial launching of the first designs, hovercraft technology was discussed and developed with the participation of representatives from shipping, aircraft, and defence industries, as well as with British Government R & D staff. Manufacturers and marketing personnel, potential builders and sellers, and not simply customers, were involved in the transformation of Cockerell's original idea into a successful marine transport technology.

In fact, technology user involvement became so extensive and influential in hovercraft's development that Cockerell himself, as a result of disputes over design directions, was dismissed from the development programme in 1966, before any substantial commercialization of the technology had taken place. Even without its inventor, hovercraft progressed through a series of incremental innovations, in response to the experience and concern of its manufacturers, distributors, and shipping company customers, to the establishment of the family of designs in operation today.[21]

The above and other case studies have depicted the important contributions of users to innovation in various industries and organizations. These analyses reveal much not only about the wide range of resources that can be tapped in implementing technical change, but also about the complex, non-mechanistic nature of that change itself, and about how management and science policy measures can foster and support a more innovative environment.

12

## Technology and Development

Although the literature on technology and development often speaks in different terms and with different emphases from that on technical change in developed economies, in many respects it reveals a similar conception of innovation, in which science and demand factors both play an important role, and in which technology users' contributions often figure prominently. The analysis of innovation in developing nations raises new concepts, such as 'technology transfer','appropriateness', 'informal sector activity', and 'indigenous capability' which can lead one to feel that technical change takes on different dimensions in a development situation. However, the new terms do not represent a departure from the central determinants of innovation, but rather a means towards a greater appreciation of the parameters of developing country economies, through which both the science and demand forces driving technical change, and the participation in that change by players from outside of the R & D institutional structure, can be more thoroughly understood and utilized.

*Early institution building*
During the 1950s and 1960s much money and effort went into the creation of centralized educational and R & D facilities in developing nations. These institutions would supply basic science, which, through an unspecified mechanism, would make discoveries that would, in turn, be channelled into industrial innovations and economic development. The institutions were established as mirror images of similar bodies in Europe and America. There was some debate about how 'basic' the focus of the new institutions should be, but all agreed that the established Western research structure should be replicated. These early years also saw a heavy investment in fixed capital in developing nations. It was assumed that, just as a university or national science organization would stimulate innovation, so would machinery, buildings, and roads provide the tools to stimulate national technical advance.

However, the expected transformation of developing countries into modern technological states did not, for the most part, occur. As Martin Bell noted,

> By the 1970s, it became clear that very few of the centralised industrial R & D organisations in developing countries were making any significant contribution to industrial development. Similarly, higher-level scientific and technological education commonly had only very weak connections with industry: results from university R & D seldom flowed into industry; and even the flow of technology embodied in university educated people was often very limited.[22]

Another problem encountered was that many people from developing countries, sent overseas to receive formal academic training that would

13

enable them to administer their national institutions, never returned to contribute to these institutions. They took on new assignments in the developed countries in which they were trained, or left their government positions to take up more lucrative private sector opportunities upon their return to their nations.

Essentially, this mode of development assistance, in supplying the structure of modern science without any coherent policy for the application of this infrastructure to the promotion of technical change, built a ship without a rudder. Bell summed up the situation very succinctly:

> the system for linking science and technology to economic development was commonly incoherent and disarticulated. ... neither the domestic structure of institutional and human resources nor the process of importing technology was generating the paths of technical, economic, and social change that had been expected.[23]

In many respects, providing for scientific infrastructure development without formulating controls and directions for the work and the application of the products of that infrastructure, was similar to a firm investing heavily in R & D without any specific technical or market goals. This science-without-policy avoided grappling with the essence of innovation, treating it instead as something that would flow from the new institutes, but could not be encouraged, or regulated.

Much of the literature on technology and development can be seen as a reaction to the limitations of this initial, ill-fated, science supply-side approach. Work in this domain seeks to better understand the innovation process within a developing country context, so that desired technical change can be better supported by government policy and action. The discussion of 'technology transfer' represents one aspect of this attempt at improving comprehension and control of innovation.

*Technology transfer*

The literature on technology transfer is vast, and this chapter will not cover its many facets.[24] Rather, it examines how work in this area has led to a greater appreciation of technical change and the importance of technology users to this process.

Martin Fransman suggests that much of the technology transfer literature from before the late 1970s displays a limited interest in technical change, in that it tends to focus on importing to achieve technical improvement, and on the choice between fixed, foreign technologies available to developing nations.[25] Its unspoken emphasis, he argues, is not on how to develop internal innovation, but on how to buy-in the products of external innovation.

On the other hand, the examination of national and local economic resources, and the appraisal of human resources in developing nations that took place alongside this discussion of the choice of products and techniques, stimulated a greater investigation and appreciation of the environment in which innovation could occur. Attention was paid not only to what countries and individuals could afford, but also to what they could produce, operate, and maintain – their 'capability'.

'Capability' has not figured prominently in discussions of innovation in industrialized nations, not because it is unimportant that new product and process formulation consider what sorts of technology can be efficiently utilized by the existing market, but because it is taken for granted that Western technology users' abilities are well understood by innovators. It became obvious that capabilities in developing countries, particularly with regard to the utilization of Western-conceived technologies, were not well understood when imported technologies failed to perform at comparable efficiencies when introduced into developing nations.

This realization inspired a more detailed analysis of capability not only in technology transfer studies, but also in other work on technology and development (some of these other areas, particularly 'appropriate technology' and 'indigenous technical knowledge' work, will be discussed later). As local capability became better appreciated, its essentially dynamic nature became more obvious and important to analysts. Their focus turned more and more to how capabilities can be adapted and enhanced as a part of the introduction of a new technology. In other words, the technology transfer literature became centrally concerned with the process of innovation within developing nations.[26] Fransman noted,

> the new focus required an analysis of the process of technological change in Third World countries rather than a more limited consideration of the costs and benefits (the latter usually excluding technological change) of transferred technology.[27]

This new focus on technological change, whether or not it represents a paradigm shift for the analysis of technology and development, or, as has been suggested above, a natural outgrowth of a greater understanding of the local technological environments in developing nations, brought the analysis of the understanding and management of innovation to centre stage in the discussion of technology transfer. Moreover, the success of technology transfer, seen in this light, depended upon the interaction between scientific potential and local capability.

*Appropriate technology*
The appropriate technology movement also was built upon the acknowledgement of the importance of local capability in the innovation process. E F Schumacher, one of the founders of this movement, wrote

> If we could turn official and popular interest away from the grandiose projects and to the real needs of the poor, the battle [for development]

15

could be won. . . . The poor can be helped to help themselves, but only by making available to them a technology that recognises the economic boundaries and limitations of poverty.[28]

Appropriate technology, as articulated by Schumacher and others, was technology that could be established within the capabilities of the environment surrounding rural poverty. This means not only that it satisfied an existing economic demand, but also that its operation and benefits could be sustained by its local users. As in the case of technology transfer, the interaction between users and the technology was a critical determinant of the technology's potential for innovation. Schumacher illustrated this importance by subtitling appropriate technology 'technology with a human face.'[29]

Unfortunately, many of the projects designed to achieve appropriate technology innovations have not performed well. As Whitcombe and Carr of the Intermediate Technology Development Group, the organization Schumacher founded to advance his ideal of appropriate technology, noted,

> examples of projects which have taken technologies beyond the pilot stage into widespread production and use are very thin on the ground. . . . even after the considerable support given to the AT movement over the past 5 years by governments and international agencies.[30]

However, this poor performance does not disprove the importance of demand factors and local capabilities to the success of innovations in rural areas, as the implementation of many appropriate technology projects failed to adhere to Schumacher's principles. Much of the new technology, like the old, was developed and tested by developed country scientists and engineers (often in developed country locations), and then presented as a fixed entity for adoption by rural users. The appropriate technologists often were less responsive to local capabilities and demand than they were to local resource availability. Rather than achieving an interactive innovation programme, in which scientific and local abilities could be united to develop a more 'human' technology, all too often the projects provided only an injection of Western science using local construction materials.

While not all innovations need to originate from user ideas, or to involve extensive user participation before their first marketing or application, earlier discussion has shown how technology users can and do play an important role in technical change in many areas. Considering the goal of the appropriate technology movement to develop products and processes that can be produced, operated, and maintained within the confines of rural capabilities, it seems likely that its approach to innovation, and that of other movements to bring the benefits of technical change to the poor in developing nations, would require user interaction in technology development in order to stand a reasonable chance of success. The investigation of indigenous technical knowledge and informal sector production activities in developing nations reveals the significant potential of user resources for the promotion of innovation.

*Indigenous technical knowledge and informal sector production*

The study of indigenous technical knowledge (ITK) has focused mainly on rural environmental and agricultural applications, while the literature concerning informal sector production (ISP) concentrates on urban, manufacturing operations.[31] While their different geographical orientations lead the two fields into different issues and discussions, both emphasize the extent to which local technology users can contribute to innovations, and both also show that users play an important role as innovators, often carrying out their own R & D work in parallel to that of official government institutions.

ITK and ISP investigations demonstrate that local farmers, artisans, and traders possess an extensive knowledge of both technical and demand factors of great importance for technology design and development, and that, in many cases, technology users provide the critical insights for the successful adaptation and introduction of new products and processes. For example, in Bangladesh farmers carried out further selection within a new hybrid rice strain in order to make it taller, in order to avoid possible damage from the wide range of paddy water levels that occur as a result of unpredictable annual rainfall.[32] As released from the research station, the hybrid strain was too short and sensitive to flood damage, which limited its appeal to farmers.

In Vietnam, a local artisan-farmer, who had been trained in the operation and maintenance of French-made dredging equipment during his twelve years of work as a mechanic in Saigon, saw that its basic impeller mechanism could be modified to undertake low-lift pumping, such as that commonly needed in rice irrigation. He developed his own impeller pump, using commercial engines and fashioning his propellers and shafts from local materials. An engine retailer in another village, apparently with no knowledge of the other innovator, came up with a similar design. Both proved very popular with local farmers, for they were cheaper and more portable than commercially available diesel pumps, and far more productive than hand pumps. Although the Vietnamese Government, the Viet Cong, and the USAID extension staff offered little support, or in some cases actively discouraged the use of the new devices, they spread rapidly through the delta farming areas, greatly transforming the upper delta agricultural economy.[33]

These case studies, and many others, show more than just user contributions to innovation. They establish that, in developing nations, much research and development occurs outside the conventional institutional backgrounds, on farms, in homes, and in workshops. This 'informal' R & D often provides key technical inputs for innovation, or generates innovations on its own.

In one part of Bangladesh, farmers surprised researchers by growing wheat on soils deemed unsuitable for that crop, using a land ridging method to conserve monsoon rainwater and therby increase the irrigated season length. The farmers had implemented their own trials of various land preparation techniques, and had decided that wheat cultivation was a viable activity. After observing this practice, the government soil scientists decided to reclassify the local soils as capable of supporting wheat, provided the farmer-developed cultivation technique.[34]

In the informal metalworking sector in Kenya, skilled artisans have developed their own cutting and forming machinery, which improves finished product quality and reduces production time and costs.[35] They, and artisans from other nations, also have formulated innovative systems both for executing work orders using available workshop staff, and for training new craftsmen.[36] Commentators on ISP differ as to whether these informal systems and the relations they establish with traders and other producers are inherently exploitative, but all admit the extensive innovation that originates within this sector.

The attention paid to the innovation process in studies of technology transfer, appropriate technology, indigenous technical knowledge, and informal sector production reflects an increased awareness on the part of those working in technology and development of the great potential of technology users for the generation and continuation of technical change. This awareness had led to the attempt, in several development fields, to tap the potential of user capabilities through the establishment of a more interactive R & D system, in which technology users play an important part in all aspects of technology development.

## Towards a More Interactive R & D–User Participation in Technology and Development

Development work in the agriculture, health, and irrigation fields today shows an increasing commitment to involving local technology users in the innovation process. This is accomplished through making users a more active partner in R & D: not limiting them to a 'guinea pig' role, but having them share in both determining research directions and priorities, and evaluating the results of trials. It cannot be said that all R & D in these areas, nor all innovation, reflects significant user participation, but several major research institutions in these fields are taking the user role in technical change very seriously. The following section examines the encouraging results of some user-interactive R & D programmes in these fields.[37]

### 1. Agriculture

At the International Potato Centre in Peru, scientists had devoted much effort to developing strains that could endure long periods of storage. They had not spoken to peasant farmers about whether declining quality through storage was a problem. This was assumed, since potatoes commonly were stored over long periods before marketing, and it was known that post-harvest losses occurred.

18

However, when they did bother to consult with local farmers, they were surprised to find that what to the researchers had seemed a critical issue was of little importance to the farmers. The farmers said that their big problem was sprouting during storage, and that the new strains were just as bad as the traditional ones in this respect. Sprouting necessitated tedious, time-consuming pruning work before potatoes could be sold or used for re-seeding, and the farmers wondered whether anything could be done about this problem. The IPC staff reorganized its research to face this new issue, and this time worked directly with the farmers to develop a diffused light storage area that significantly reduced sprouting.[38] By themselves, the technicians invented much, but innovated little. In tandem with the farmers, they addressed more important problems, and found solutions.

The International Centre for Tropical Agriculture (CIAT) in Colombia also has initiated interactive research efforts. There, they are pursuing an assessment of the interactive research method itself, through an examination of the effects of including farmer inputs to experimental design and management to the outcomes of fertilizer trials.[39] The initial results have shown that, at least in the area of research design, allowing the farmers a say in what is tested and how comparisons are to be made is beneficial, as it has helped to find and test the merits of promising mixtures of traditionally used manures and new chemical fertilizers.

Fertilizer trials have been a source of interactive research development in Africa, too. In Nigeria it was found that the best crop results were obtained by combining the 'modern' input of fertilizer with farmers' traditional methods of crop management.[40] This interactive innovation outperformed the combination of the fertilizer with 'improved' cultivation practices suggested by the local FAO team. The potential of local knowledge, particularly of inter-cropping methods, to benefit agricultural improvement projects has also been noted in East Africa.[41]

Paul Richards, drawing on years of agricultural experience in West Africa, argues that the whole approach to agricultural development needs to be overhauled, with peasant farmers given far greater power and influence over research directions. Their capacities can be channelled into production far better if they are placed in a dominant role:

> It is precisely on evidence of this sort: the ability of West African smallholders to get best results from a combination of (so-called) 'modern' and 'traditional' techniques, that the case for the 'populist' strategy rests. Science . . . should be the servant not the master of this kind of inventiveness.[42]

There is some reason for believing that interactive agricultural R & D and a far greater user role in innovation may be coming to the fore. The International Development Research Centre recently conducted seminars and issued a large publication devoted to the analysis of farmers' participation in the development of agricultural technology.[43]

## 2. Health

The health area exhibits perhaps the greatest commitment to interactive R & D and the user role in technical change of any development field, with the World Health Organization (WHO) making the utilization of traditional knowledge and techniques a priority in health care development in its Alma-Ata declaration of 1978.[44] Halfden Mahler, WHO's Director General, has noted that, in order to meet the organization's goal of adequate primary health care for all by the year 2000,

> all useful methods will have to be employed and all possible resources utilized – Among these methods are various kinds of indigenous practices; and among those resources are various types of traditional practitioners and birth attendants.[45]

The WHO even produces volumes on how to incorporate traditional medicine into health care research, administration, and training.[46]

Population control and family planning have been among the most difficult and controversial areas of health development work. Perhaps because of this, these areas show a great interest in user-dominated innovation strategies. Some of their researchers argue that, just as many industrial areas show companies with the greatest marketing skills winning out through better understanding of user needs, the success of population control campaigns may come to depend on keeping in touch with and responding to local family planning attitudes. Several recent articles in this area concentrate on the potential of marketing research methods from the commercial sector, such as focus group research, for guiding family planning programmes onto a more successful course.[47]

## 3. Irrigation

Even the very applied science-focused field of irrigation is devoting greater attention to user involvement in technology development. Ruttan writes that in India, irrigation work is now moving away from its former emphasis on hardware and physical analysis to focus more on local management capabilities and operations concerns.[48] The failure to link engineering developments to corresponding management innovations is seen as a major constraint in many projects.

Max Lowdermilk, an irrigation and water management specialist for USAID in India, argues that the key to improved irrigation management lies in greater farmer involvement. He points out that farmers possess knowledge of local topography, soil types, and other physical parameters important to irrigation system development. He also notes that farmers can identify social constraints to certain irrigation options, saving a project from implementing a system that will not be supported by local communities. Moreover, where farmers feel they have played a role in the design and implementation of irrigation systems, they take a more active and effective role in the maintenance of these systems. Lowdermilk points to this factor as a key to the success of the *warabundi* system in North India, in which farmers and irrigation authorities work closely together and share the responsibility for sustaining a continuous water supply. In poorer performing systems, on the other hand, farmers reported that the lack of good communications with irrigation authorities was a major problem, particularly the absence of information about canal closures for maintenance and repair.[49]

The incorporation of a more user-interactive R & D operation into work in technology and development makes that work better informed as to the technical and economic parameters that determine the success or failure of new products and processes. Knowledge of local user capabilities both establishes the technical and demand constraints within which the innovation must operate, and identifies resources from outside of the standard R & D institutional system that can assist in the design and development of new technologies. Therefore, a user-involved R & D strategy seems more likely to consistently produce appropriate, successful innovations.

In this respect, those institutions that adopt a more interactive R & D approach are behaving much in the same manner as those industrial firms, such as IBM, Boeing, Pillsbury, and Howard, that have recognized technology users as an important asset for sustaining technical advance and competitiveness. In the development area, as in the industrial sphere, an organization's knowledge of its environment and its resources is a fundamental component of its ability to produce and successfully introduce innovations.

It is not surprising that, given the expanding interest in the process of technical change, and the importance of the interaction between R & D institutions and their external environments in this process, that the study of communications has provided useful insights into innovation. Communications research, in analyzing the introduction of new technologies in both industrial and development situations, has enhanced understanding of the key players in innovation, and of the types of participation that are essential to this process.

## Communications Research

There are two principal dimensions to the investigation of the role of communications in innovation. The first is the analysis of the flow of information and knowledge within the R & D system, and between that system and its external environment, that contributes to the development of technologies. The second is the observation of the process of introducing new products and techniques into the market, noting the actions that influence the diffusion of innovations throughout their target populations.

The work of Thomas Allen and his colleagues has provided some of the most important insights on information flows and their effects on technology development.[50] Allen's essential contribution has been to point out that information exchange is not an even process, and that, within firms, certain individuals show a greater propensity to search out and transmit data and ideas than do others. Allen terms such individuals 'gatekeepers', for, in many respects, they provide the key to technology development within their firms.

Gatekeepers attract and provide information concerning both the scientific and market demand factors that are the central determinants of the fate of innovation. 'Technological gatekeepers' are staff who maintain greater contact with developments in their technical field, both through paying special attention to published research results and through having frequent conversations, correspondence, and other less formal linkages with fellow researchers. 'Marketing gatekeepers' keep in touch with the experiences of new product and process launches, and with popular opinions and needs that bear demand implications for technology development.

Allen demonstrates that firms which recognize the roles of their gate-keepers, and which seek to facilitate gatekeepers' information collection activities and their transmission of their findings to other staff, encourage successful innovation. In a particularly striking example, he describes the marked improvement in the technology development work of a firm that altered its internal office architecture in order to provide a more central, accessible position for its technological gatekeeper.[51]

The importance of key players and differences in capabilities within communities are also cited in the findings of research on technology diffusion. Diffusion studies, typified by the work of Everett Rogers and his colleagues, note that both the willingness to adopt new products and techniques, and the influence of individual adoption actions, are not equally distributed among a sample population.

Within any community there exists a variation in the eagerness to adopt new products and processes. Rogers identifies different categories of adopters, ranging from the most immediately receptive ('innovators' and 'early adopters') to the more resistant to change ('late majority' and 'laggards'). He records the economic and personal characteristics of individuals who most often fit into these various categories.[52] Understanding the nature and propensities of the different adopter groups allows for greater prediction of how a given innovation will diffuse throughout a population. Equally important, it enables one to evaluate the compatibility of an innovation within both the technical and economic constraints governing a community, by noting to what extent adoption is occurring within the average types that comprise the bulk of its market.

Rogers also points out that opinion is a powerful force behind all technical change, and that certain individuals wield far greater influence over local opinion than do others. He describes the characteristics of 'opinion leaders', and demonstrates the importance of utilizing these leaders to the successful diffusion of innovations.[53] The important lesson drawn from this discussion is that being able to identify and incorporate opinion leaders into the process of technical change is a central determinant of the fate of an innovation.

While the study of technology diffusion has provided important insights, it also has encumbered the analysis of innovation with a significant and unnecessary limitation. The premise that appears to underlie much of Rogers' and his colleagues' work is that diffusion is a process that follows after technology development, and therefore, to a large extent, the types of communication and interaction that occur in diffusion have little to offer the innovation process. Communication and interaction between researchers and potential adopters, while discussed in detail as a part of diffusion, is not assessed as a potentially important element of innovation itself. As Barnett *et al* have pointed out in a critique of Rogers, it may not be important that villagers have a say in all technology design and development, but there certainly exist cases in which their involvement in this earlier, formative process is essential to successful innovation.[54] It is difficult to see how villagers could contribute to the choice of chemicals in birth control pills in Korea (an example used by Rogers); but that does not mean that they could not make valuable inputs into the development of other technologies, particularly those in areas such as agriculture, which are sensitive to the specifics of local environments.

The flaw in the Rogers-type approach is that it envisages a mechanistic, linear process of innovation, one in which technology is handed down in completed form from R & D to users. It appears that Rogers himself has become dissatisfied with the applications of such a mechanistic model, as his recent writings urge a more dynamic approach to the communications field, and speak of a passing out from under the influence of old paradigms. In one work he even remarks, 'Perhaps the diffusion of technological innovations will cease to be a central issue in the 'new development'.'[55]

The study of innovation in both industrial and development situations, whose findings concerning the importance of user interaction in technology development were discussed earlier, demonstrates the inadequacy of this linear, mechanistic model for predicting and managing the process of technical change. It is being persuasively argued that non-linear, organic models are necessary for understanding and directing innovation, models that dissolve this hierarchical conception of R & D and user roles.

## Non-Linear Innovation and Its Management

Some of the most exciting new work in the analysis of innovation has been that which challenges the capability of the existing economic framework to adequately explain firm and industry behaviour. At the heart of this critique lies the dismantling of a linear conception of technical change. Nelson and Winter demonstrate the inadequacy of trying to treat firm and industry development as a continual motion towards a maximization of given factors.[56] As an alternative, they propose an 'evolutionary' model of economic change, in which a firm's interaction with its environment, and with other firms, presents a variety of forces, and can give rise to a variety of survival strategies.[57] This interaction and adaptation to an environment, that is itself changing over time, mirrors the phenomenon of species change as a result of natural selection, (hence the 'evolutionary' nature of the model).

Stephen J. Kline points out that in a given innovation process, the object of that innovation, rather than always passing from research, to development, to production and, finally, to marketing in a continuous progression, often enters, departs, and returns to these stages repeatedly, in the course of the overall creative and adaptive design experience.[58] The process derives its energy not merely from initial creative impetus, but also from feedback between the sectors of the firm, as the influences of technical and demand considerations raised by a variety of sources come into play.

Academic and corporate R & D, while an important element of innovation, is not its sole impetus. A technology may require many adaptations during the course of its design and development in order to acquire the attributes of a successful innovation, and some of these adaptations can only be effected outside of the confines of the R & D system (although such adaptations can involve the participation of R & D personnel, acting outside of their traditional environment). As Kim Clark has written,

> Each of the phases of development involves the search for solutions to problems, but the nature of the problems, the nature of solutions and the nature of the search process are quite different. The implication is that the environment for innovation, the set of skills, incentives, and organizational context required for effective action, will differ as well. Where fresh insight and bold creativity may be required in laying down an 'architecture', stability, consistency, and planning may be the essentials in the 'regular' phase movement down the hierarchy.[59]

Since the requirements for innovation can change over time, a central goal of innovation management should be the maintenance of as wide a portfolio of skills as possible as a part of the overall makeup of an organization. The organization, in order to have access to the particular resources that could provide the key to the development of a technology, has to make itself open to contributions not only from within its technical staff, but also from the capabilities of technology users who operate outside its walls. As Rosabeth Moss Kanter points out,

> when a company innovates in practices which ensure that more kinds of people, at all levels, have the skills and opportunity to contribute to solving problems and suggesting new ideas, then it is establishing the context for further innovations. Improved organization designs and human-resource practices can be a company's *innovation-producing innovations* [emphasis hers].[60]

24

Kanter's insights are valuable on two levels. On the level of the firm, they point out that those companies that excel in human resource management also excel in innovation. On the institutional level, they stress that R & D structures that are open to outside contributions and discourse harness greater resources for innovation than those which are separated from user involvement by administrative or other barriers.

*Firm management*

Even in industries in which technical advances are rapid and scientific concerns dominate, extra-R & D contributions can be essential to successful technical change. Shanklin and Ryans' study of innovation within 'high-technology' industries shows that, while creativity may be the sole component of initial success, sustained competitiveness depends upon linking that creativity to the knowledge of demand factors found outside of company R & D personnel, in its marketing department. They comment that marketing-R & D linkage should be concerned 'not only with market planning, but also with offering directions for new research and application.'[61]

The importance of establishing an interactive relationship between R & D and external knowledge sources, such as marketing staffs, is epitomized in Gardiner and Rothwell's study of the competitive performance of British Leyland and Ford in the compact car market in the UK. Leyland's initial model employed a radical new technology that had distinct advantages over the hardware of its Ford equivalent. However, over time the Ford organization, responding to ongoing technical and market evaluation of its offerings, made numerous incremental improvements to the design of its cars. Leyland did not exhibit a similar responsiveness to market feedback in its own R & D efforts.

> Despite the BL 1100/1300 series incorporating a number of radical innovations (transverse engine and transmision, hydrostatic suspension) it failed, in the longer-term, to keep abreast of the technologically more conventional [Ford] Cortina series: the little-changed 1100/1300 series became increasingly uncompetitive with a substantially improved Cortina series.[62]

The authors also cite Ford's commitment to 'makeability' in its designs, by which they mean its integration of production line concerns with the work of its R & D system.[63] The overall Ford innovation strategy marshalled more resources to assist its design efforts, and, given BL's relative lack of attention to extra-R & D resources, it is not surprising that Ford consistently outperformed BL during the 1960s and 1970s.

*R & D institution management*

The innovativeness of the work of national R & D institutions also is greatly enhanced by involving them more with external sources of knowledge and skills. Unfortunately, governments tend to establish institutional

25

structures and relationships which, rather than opening up research to receive contributions from these sources, serve to isolate it even further from the inputs of technology users. This institutional isolation is a particular problem in much R & D within developing nations.

Norman Clark's analysis of the institutional elements of rural technology generation in developing countries points out that lines of information and authority tend to interpose ministerial structures between R & D organizations and technology users. In this technology development structure (see Figure 2.2 below), technical possibilities are not communicated to users directly by scientists and engineers, but indirectly through the intermediary role of often less knowledgeable, less formally-educated extension agents. These agents receive the technical inputs as part of packages put together by their ministries, using raw scientific material provided by the research institutes.[64]

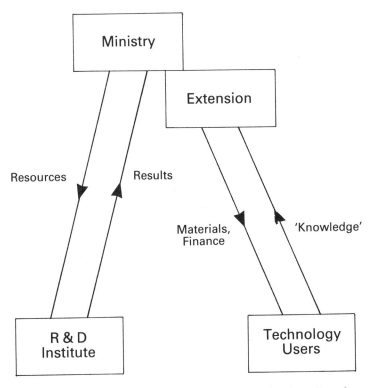

Figure 2.2 *Typical Institutional Relationships for Technology Development: 'Hierarchical' Model*

This system possesses serious practical problems in terms of utilization of scarce time and resources.[65] From an innovation standpoint, its central flaw is the barrier it creates between the R & D and the productive sectors of the economy. Technology users often cannot obtain sufficient knowledge of the operating principles and potential of the package from the extension agents, in order to incorporate it into the conditions and constraints of their existing agricultural systems. Likewise, the researchers often do not receive sufficient information about the needs of these systems and the operating experience of R & D products in order to carry out necessary re-design of hardware and re-thinking of research programmes. As Herrera notes, 'the body of empirical knowledge of the traditional sector has practically no connection with the R and D systems of the modern parts of society. It is not considered, in general, an object of scientific enquiry.[66] The potential of both the 'conventional' scientific training of the researchers and the 'non-conventional' indigenous expertise of the users to interact in the generation of innovations is suppressed by this communications barrier.

Clark points out that an alternative structure, in which communications across the scientific, ministerial, and productive sectors is facilitated is now

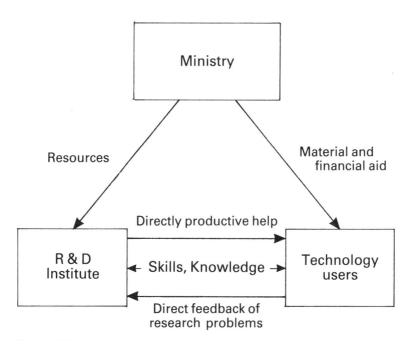

Figure 2.3 *Institutional Relationships for User-Interactive Innovation: 'Biological' Model*

coming to be explored in the agricultural technology development area.[67] This structure (see Figure 2.3 above) still involves links from the Ministry to both research and production, but these links become far less important than the feedback relationship between the latter two sectors. The resources of government finance and personnel assist the innovation process, but its heart lies in the interaction between scientists and users in technology development. Clark comments,

> Here we have something akin to a 'biological' model of social development in which scientific and technological activities lend a continuous dynamic to the productive process which itself throws up scientific problems requiring feedback to the research system in a continuous series of linkages.[68]

It is appropriate that the interactive, evolutionary process of technical change is best fostered by an institutional structure that reflects a biological basis of organization.[69]

The experience of the International Rice Research Institute (IRRI) in generating successful innovations in agricultural equipment technology exemplifies the value of this more interactive, 'biological' organization. The IRRI agricultural implement programme, which has succeeded in introducing several new technologies, such as its rotary weeder, to self-sustaining commercial manufacture and utilization throughout Southeast Asia and in other parts of the world, has been a user-interactive effort. Ronald Black, who played a leading role in the development of IRRI's programme, notes that a key feature of its work, one that distinguishes it from that of most other (less successful) agricultural equipment design in developing nations,

> is the close and continuous relationship that the IRRI staff members maintain with Philippine [its host country] metal-working firms. This consists of much more than visiting a firm as part of an extension strategy to have a new design commercialized. IRRI staff is continually dropping in on metalworking firms to exchange ideas and see what is happening. These visits are now in both directions with industry people visiting IRRI, perhaps as much as vice versa.[70]

If IRRI, an organization working on the frontiers of global agricultural technology, feels it owes its success, in large part, to its interaction with manufacturers, it stands to reason that other R & D organizations could also profit from opening themselves further to inputs from technology users in other sectors of the economy.

## User Interaction in Energy Development

It also would seem likely that pursuing a more interactive R & D strategy would yield good results for innovation in other technology areas and, in particular, in the area of energy technology. Energy has more users than any other product, as every individual (and every organism, for that

**Table 2.1 The Economic and Technical Performance of Nuclear Plant**

| | USA | West Germany | France | Canada |
|---|---|---|---|---|
| *Operating Performance* | BWRs & PWRs mediocre overall, but several consistently good units as well as many erratic performers | BWRs: major repairs required to all but most recent reactors to meet new safety standards. Performance originally poor, but now good PWRs: now outstanding | PWRs: performance good although there have been a number of generic problems | CANDU performance outstandingly good although a serious technical problem affecting the two oldest units may have implications for the later units |
| Average Load Factor[1] 1975–84 (%) | PWR: 58.6 BWR: 55.9 | PWR: 76.5 BWR: 35.2 | PWR: 67.5 | CANDU: 81.4 |
| *Construction Times*[2] | Very long with only a few exceptions. Contributing factors include site problems, design changes and cash shortage | Long overall planning time but construction phase reasonably short | Short construction times although extending somewhat in recent years as larger reactors are ordered | Reasonably short although low demand growth is resulting in voluntary extensions |
| *Construction Costs*[2] | Very high with a few exceptions, and a powerful tendency to increase in real terms over the years | Relatively high, partly due to rigorous safety requirements and partly due to design changes during construction | Low and showing only limited tendency to increase in real terms | Originally seemed relatively high, but very limited increase in real terms means that costs now seem reasonably low |

1. Load factor is a measure of the actual electrical output produced as a proportion of the maximum output at design rating.
2. No quantitative measures of construction time and cost are presented here because all measurements are subject, especially in international comparisons, to very serious qualifications.
*Source:* MacKerron and Thomas

matter) requires it to exist. Therefore, energy technology development should have the greatest user knowledge and skill resources to draw upon. However, the energy field, as a whole, has shown little interest in or application of user contributions, with its work dominated by insular research and an attitude that, if fuel and the means to use it can be supplied by science, economic problems will be solved. This is an attitude that virtually ignores innovation, postulating essentially that invention will automatically bring progress.

However, recent work on the nuclear power sector by staff of the Science Policy Research Unit indicates that user-related issues may be of great concern to the energy field. Gordon MacKerron and Steve Thomas's research on nuclear reactor performance shows significant variation in reactor efficiency (based on average load factors) both within and between nations, and a significant variation in the efficiency of operation of the one basic pressurized water reactor design (PWR) used in many installations in the United States, West Germany, and France. Their results for the latter are summarized in Table 2.1 above.

MacKerron and Thomas note that, while global variations are difficult to explain, 'because of the extreme difficulty of isolating particular requirements in so complex and interdependent an industry,' user factors may figure strongly in the comparative performances of the three pressurized water reactor-dependent nations:

> the variability of performance in what, for three of the countries, is essentially the same technology, does point to the importance of the contribution of the user or customer, namely the utility. . . . What does seem to be necessary in a utility is a capacity for technical leadership of nuclear projects and an ability to manage and control the various activities involved, whether these are provided in-house, or sub-contracted to other parties such as architect-engineers.[71]

The extent and quality of user involvement in reactor development seems to directly correlate to reactor performance. MacKerron and Thomas emphasize the role of such user involvement in the high performance CANDU reactors operated by the Ontario Hydro company.[72] Their study concludes,

> there does seem to be one dominant requirement for good technical and economic performance. This is the technically informed and well-managed involvement of the customer – the utility – in all the major aspects of this most complex technology. It is perhaps also worth saying that this conclusion is consistent with the findings of much other research on innovation in sophisticated capital goods industries, that strong customer involvement, and good producer-customer relationships, are essential ingredients of success.[73]

If users play such an important role in the nuclear energy field, it is likely that their role is equally important for innovation in other fuel technologies.

Users certainly can play a key role in the renewable energy area, particularly in the development of forest energy technologies. The following chapters provide a detailed examination of lessons from the development of renewable energy technologies for developing countries, with particular attention paid to the experience of a user-involved innovation approach for forest energy development pursued by the Energy Research Council of Sudan. They reveal the limitations of attempts to establish energy innovations through the construction and installation of technologies on demonstration sites within R & D institutes or in the field. Such a 'technical fix' approach, which has not involved users in the process of technology development, has not been able to achieve widespread production and adoption of renewable energy technologies, and therefore has not generated successful innovation.

The chapters to come also show the specific and important contributions that can be made to innovation by the skills and knowledge of a wide range of technology users, including artisans, farmers, villagers, and urban housewives. They describe how changes in the way in which a research institution pursues its work, bringing it into closer contact with technology users, help to make its work more innovative, and hence more successful.

# CHAPTER THREE
# Renewable Energy and Development Assistance

The principal renewable energy areas and applications have been well covered in the literature of the past decade. There are four main sources of renewable energy: solar radiation, wind, flowing water, and biomass. Grouping all these sources under the one heading of 'renewable' or 'new and renewable' creates some ambiguity, as some, like solar radiation and wind, are virtually inexhaustible, while others, like wood, are very exhaustible – in fact, it is the latter's scarcity, rather than its abundance, that is often the motivation for work on technology development. Also, coal, oil, and gas, all 'conventional' or 'commercial' fuels excluded from this categorization are, in a physical sense, renewable, although on a longer, geological time scale. Perhaps the most accurate way to describe the above grouping of renewable energy resources is to say that it represents those fuels for whom one of the following is the case: either

1) their supply cannot be significantly depleted within one or two human generations, or
2) this supply can be significantly increased during that same time period.

Renewable energy resources can be tapped in a wide variety of ways, which can be roughly categorized as thermal, mechanical, and electrical energy production. Thermal energy production is exemplified in such diverse technologies as solar water heating, wood-burning stoves, and afforestation for fuelwood production. Mechanical energy can be obtained directly from renewable energy sources, as in the case of windmills or waterwheels. It can also be obtained indirectly, through the prior conversion of a renewable energy resource into a fuel suitable for shaft or other power machinery, as in the case of producer gas, biogas (methane produced from biomass), or alcohol fuel-powered devices. Electrical energy can be produced through direct transformation of renewable resources in photovoltaic cells, or through renewable fuel-powered equipment, such as wind turbines, steam turbines, or producer gas-fed diesel generators.

The preceding paragraphs present only a small part of the wide variety of renewable fuels and applications developed through work on technology alternatives to petroleum-based energy production and use. This research has involved an equally wide variety of scientific and technological disciplines, covering the realms of biology, chemistry, physics, and engineering.

The renewable energy area, not surprisingly, embraces a great diversity of professional interest and prejudice. Its sole unifying element is its reliance on energy resources whose regeneration can take place on a human time scale, unlike the regenerative processes required for petroleum and coal. While all present energy resources are recycled and recreated over geological time, only sun, wind, hydro, and biomass-based fuel supplies can be managed on a self-sustaining basis within the lifetimes of their human users.

*The potential of renewable energy technologies for developing countries*
Many of the works that describe the promise of renewable energy also note its particular attractiveness for developing countries. Unlike conventional energy resources, which are in short supply in many of these nations, renewable resources are, in theory, available to all. Moreover, most developing nations are located within the tropical zone, which possesses generally higher solar and biomass (in the form of tropical forest) resources than the rest of the world.

The promotion of renewable energy assistance programmes has been founded on the premise that the development of resources and technologies for energy production can address three of the major politico-economic issues facing poorer countries today: foreign exchange scarcity, deprivation of rural and urban poor, and environmental decay. Domestic renewable resources can be developed to substitute, in large part, for petroleum imports, saving foreign exchange and improving trade balances. Because sun, wind, and biomass are readily available in rural areas, their exploitation can remedy problems caused by the absence of adequate transport infrastructure to deliver commercial fuels for rural agricultural and household needs. Moreover, as their supply cannot be influenced by external political sources, their increasing exploitation will correspondingly increase both local and national self-reliance, reducing dependency on fuel-exporting nations. In addition, the movement towards a renewable fuel focus will entail a movement away from the current system of environmental destruction and agricultural land degradation, as biomass production comes to dominate over deforestation.

## Renewable Energy Development Programmes: Performance Problems

As a 1985 review of USAID renewable energy activities in Asia points out, the last ten years have seen the creation of 'high quality, indigenous centers of RET design and adaptation,' and some renewable energy technologies have become the technologies-of-choice for meeting rural agricultural and other demands in certain areas.[1] However, while individual accomplishments have demonstrated the viability of certain technologies, there is scepticism as to whether the overall effort in renewable energy has been

33

effective in inducing innovation in energy production and consumption patterns, and in improving the lot of the poor through this innovation. Numerous analyses of specific renewable energy programmes have cited failures to achieve projected physical and economic outputs, both due to technical shortcomings and to socio-economic constraints.[2] Yet, it has been difficult to gain a sense of overall performance, and of donors' own impressions as to the strengths and weaknesses of their technology development strategies.

One of the main reasons it has been difficult to evaluate overall project progress and donors' reactions to date is simply that most donors do not make evaluation material widely available. Much of the evaluation materials produced by both national and multilateral donors are classified, and hence unavailable for review outside of these organizations. Also, as Barnett points out, much of the public domain material sent to donors and developing country governments regarding the choice and evaluation of renewable energy technologies has been coloured by self-interest, and thus is not particularly useful in gauging either technology performance or donor opinions.[3]

The one donor that can be monitored more easily is the United States Agency for International Development which, under the public disclosure provisions of U.S. law, has to make all its policy decisions and evaluations available for public view. While on an individual project level it would be difficult to generalize from USAID's experience, it is likely that reviews of its regional or global activities, which span a wide variety of nations, ecosystems, technologies, and project designs, will provide a reasonably accurate picture of the general progress of renewable energy technologies. The American experience, by its size and scope, should reflect the larger donor experience.

The analysis of USAID's own evaluations to come does not imply that extensive knowledge of innovation problems did not exist within this or other donor organizations before their publication from 1984 to 1986. The evaluations constitute a public confirmation of this prior knowledge and, because of their political influence, enhance the likelihood that institute-wide policy actions will be taken to address these problems.

## The US Government's appraisal of its renewable energy programme

From 1978 to 1986 the US Government, through USAID, provided $304 million in support of 86 renewable energy projects.[4] In 1982 it published its first official evaluation of project performance on a regional level, the General Accounting Office's review of African programmes. The GAO, the government's independent auditing and accounting body, expressed great concern over two main features of the programmes it reviewed: failure to adhere to implementation schedules, and the field testing of technologies with questionable economic potential.[5] In supporting the latter concern, the GAO cited USAID staff members' comments at its African Energy workshop of April 1982.[6]

Perhaps influenced by the GAO report, USAID commissioned its own reviews of its energy activities, producing three major reports between 1984 and 1986. The Bureau for Africa published *Renewable Energy Technologies in Africa: An Assessment of Field Experience and Future Directions* in April 1984. The Bureau for Asia, jointly with the Office of Energy, released its *Renewable Energy Systems Installed in Asia: Current Successes and the Potential for Future Widespread Dissemination* in April 1985. Finally, the agency's own Inspector General completed its *Audit of AID Renewable Energy Projects* in February 1986, considering the previous reviews and including independent evaluations by the office of the assistant inspector general for audit.[7]

The three critical appraisals of the USAID renewable energy programme express varying levels of concern, but all agree that work to date has had limited success, and that the present renewable energy development strategy needs to be modified. The 1982 GAO report cautioned that its review took place at a relatively early stage of project implementation, and only involved a Washington-based document analysis. Nonetheless, it pointed out that the serious discrepancies between project targets and actual outputs already existed, with 24 of the 28 African missions' projects behind in their implementation schedules.[8] It concluded that, consistent with its earlier findings in a study of USAID forestry activities, 'to avoid delays and serious implementation problems, AID project planning must be more realistic in assessing the capabilities and limitations of developing countries.[9]

The two later studies, carried out with USAID itself, were more direct and harsh in their criticism. The Africa Bureau summary of its 1984 findings included the following negative assessments:

> Renewable energy technologies, systems and related professional and technical training appear to be inadequately matched to national energy requirements and end-user needs. . . .
> The marketing/dissemination of renewable energy systems and equipment for agricultural and rural development is currently ineffective.[10]

By 1986, the USAID Inspector General's office found even stronger words to use in its report:

> AID has followed a technology demonstration approach to renewable energy since the program began in 1977. Under this approach technologies were researched, tested and developed with little consideration for application or intended end user needs. Resulting technologies generally proved unsuited or inappropriate for specific energy problems.[11]

All three reports regarded the basic demonstration strategy employed by USAID's renewable energy projects to be a poor method for achieving sustained innovation in the energy sector in developing nations.

35

*Failure to address user needs*
As the Africa Bureau pointed out, by 1984 the available data indicated that several of the technologies perform quite well, even under harsh environmental conditions. However,

> overall systems cost-effectiveness and social acceptability limits the number of renewable energy technology options for consideration as candidates for widespread application in Africa. . . . Renewable energy technologies and systems under development may not address end-user priority needs.[12]

Two major problems were exposed here. USAID's own energy staff doubted that many of the technologies it had supported were affordable to the people they sought to benefit, as the GAO had speculated two years before. But even more important, USAID was stating that, regardless of cost-effectiveness, the technologies did not address the priority needs of the rural poor. African rural peasants, most of whom were engaged in agriculture, needed better transport for goods and services to and from their villages, and low-cost ways to reduce labour constraints during soil preparation – but these functions were not amongst the capabilities of the bulk of renewable energy technologies under demonstration.[13]

In essence, the three reports depicted the failings of an insular, technically-fixated R & D effort. Although this effort had come up with hardware that, in many cases, could work in the field, its products failed to address or to solve the specific energy problems they encountered. To a large extent, much of the work from 1978 to 1986 had assumed that providing energy, or providing a means to exploit a renewable resource, would solve people's problems. What was found was that technical fixes that did not accommodate local needs did not succeed in solving local problems, no matter how clever and efficient their designs. The renewable energy sector, in this sense, was making the same discoveries made by analysts of industrial innovation and other development professionals.

While the recognition of the importance of need factors and greater involvement with technology users in the official USAID literature is an encouraging political development, there is a disturbing aspect to these documents. It appears that there has been no transfer of this sort of knowledge to the renewable energy sector from the agriculture, irrigation, and health areas, which grappled with need and user participation issues long before renewable energy became a serious interest of the organization. The energy sector of USAID has carried out its initial programme development without profiting from the experience of these older assistance sectors, and repeated many of their mistakes.

*Limited technology replication*
In 1986, USAID's Inspector General concluded, 'Most of AID's prior renewable energy projects will not be replicated'.[14] Some of the obstacles

to replication were contained in the limited consideration of the needs of the rural poor. But, although the Inspector General did not employ the phrase 'user needs' in any other sense than this, his discussion of the problem of replication revealed another aspect of the user role in technical change not addressed by USAID's projects. This was the participation of other 'users', those who construct and distribute technologies, in the innovation process. Without this sort of participation, replication could not take place.

The core of USAID's replication problem, the Inspector General pointed out, lay in the organization's failure even to include a consideration of this goal in project design. 'Twenty-one, or 88 per cent, of the 24 project papers reviewed lacked replication planning.'[15] Projects concentrated on the construction and testing of prototypes, without considering how larger numbers of technologies could be produced, or how well these technologies could be operated and maintained under typical field use conditions.

The Inspector General cited a USAID rice hull fuel project as an example of this type of short-sightedness, criticizing it for installing the prototype in a large government rice mill, where conditions bore little relation to those in the smaller private mills that accounted for the bulk of rice production.[16] USAID Energy and Asia Bureau officials, responding to this criticism, stated 'A government owned rice mill was used to assess the cost effectiveness of rice hulls as an energy source because it was more conducive to project success than privately owned mills.'[17] Such a response served only to confirm the Inspector General's point, as it made it seem that the entire project was devoted to adjusting the user environment to ensure the successful performance of the hardware, rather than trying to develop a technology that would meet the needs of the rice producers in the country. The Inspector General's response to this objection was to use it as fuel for his own argument:

> This example illustrates the technology driven approach to renewable energy projects that AID has followed since the program began. The primary objective of the project was to test and demonstrate the rice hull technology with little consideration for the needs of intended users or the replication and commercialization potential of the technology. As a result, the project tested and demonstrated a technology that was too expensive, unsuited to needs of intended users and lacking in replication potential.[18]

### The Asia Bureau report

The USAID Asia and Energy Bureau study, completed in 1985, from its very title, (containing the phrase 'current successes and the potential for future widespread dissemination') suggested an optimism in sharp contrast to the criticism and pessimism of the earlier studies. To a large extent this was due not to a significant difference in results for Asian renewable energy projects, which were to receive equally poor marks in the Inspector General's report, but rather to the different purpose of the study itself. The consultant hired for this investigation was preparing a background paper for a planned review meeting of regional USAID energy officers, who were interested to know which, of all the technologies supported by their programme, showed the greatest promise.[19] They could then concentrate future project planning on supporting these technologies, which was likely to generate the highest outputs per unit USAID input.

The consultant reviewed a selection of projects involving seven renewable energy technologies chosen by USAID as 'representative of the progress and potential of such systems in Asia.[20] His summary of his findings contained not a single negative reference to any of the renewable energy work he examined during a ten week trip to four countries. Clearly, he regarded his mission not as one of 'assessment', which implies an objective review of the technologies, but as one of description of the attributes of success.

This is certainly the view taken by the Inspector General of this study, for when the Energy Bureau objected to the pessimism of his 1986 findings by citing the promise described in the consultant's report on Asian projects, the following exchange occurred'

*Management [Energy Bureau] Comments*
A recent evaluation by the Bureau for Asia and Near East identified several technologies which have begun widespread dissemination and others with dissemination potential.

*Office of the Inspector General Comments*
After 8 years of experimentation and expenditures of $170 million [the total amount involved in the projects reviewed in his sample], AID should be well into disseminating proven replicable technologies rather than considering potential.[21]

Considered by itself, the latter remark could be construed as unfair, as many successful technologies in energy and other sectors have taken far longer than eight years from initial development to widespread replication. However, the Inspector General was not considering the matter in isolation, but in specific reference to Section 106 of the US Government's Foreign Assistance Act, which stressed that technologies to be supported should already possess replication potential, and that projects should be developed and implemented 'in a timely manner,'[22] The 'successes' cited in the Asia report were not successes from the standpoint of USAID's obligations under the larger legislative mandate through which it was authorized to support renewable energy development.

The Asia study did not, therefore, dispute the findings of other evaluations of USAID's renewable energy work, but looked at this work on a more micro-level. Moreover, within its individual project focus, it confirmed the importance of the user role in successful innovation.

The study found five factors that characterized the most successful of the diverse technologies examined. Their development patterns showed:

1) high value attached to system output;
2) participation by end-users in system adaptation or construction;
3) good local resource base (physical resource);
4) compatibility with existing local fabricating facilities; and
5) relative inexpensiveness when compared with other methods for doing the same work.[23]

Interestingly, four of these five factors cited were user-based, while the fifth was not technology, but environment-determined. In this respect the consultant's report supported the other reports' contention that user involvement should be given priority in technology development. The most successful projects examined contained a wide variety of user involvement in technology development. This variety not only included the accommodation of consumer need and financial capability, but also the participation of users as both manufacturers and technology designers. Clearly, users played an important role in aiding successful innovation not only through adopting technologies once they had been released from the R & D system, but also in helping to form these technologies from their initial stages of development.

## Forest Energy Technologies

USAID's analysis of its own project experience illustrates that renewable energy development assistance has been hampered by an excessively technology-driven approach. Work on forest energy technologies, for the most part, has contained the same bias, and has confronted the same problems that have inhibited the general progress of the renewable energy field. The following discussion examines how some of the major problems facing the development of three forest energy technologies – charcoal production, improved wood-burning stoves, and forestry – reflect an absence of an understanding of user demands and of user participation in technology development.

### 1 Charcoal production

The central issue that has inspired all work in charcoal production concerns the waste of wood energy involved in the conversion of firewood to charcoal. The vast majority of publications in this field have focused upon this technical problem, investigating how changes to kiln design can increase the overall energy efficiency of the carbonization process.[24] Such studies have shown, without doubt, that both changes in kiln materials and the incorporation of gaseous and liquid carbonization product recovery processes into the combustion system can significantly reduce the energy losses now present in charcoal making.

However, as Gerald Foley has noted,

> In the majority of cases, the attempts made in the past to introduce new technologies have had little, if any, lasting impact on traditional charcoal making practices. Even where the new technologies have had an initial success, they have tended to be abandoned when the project promoters leave.[25]

While industrial charcoal producers in a few countries (Brazil and Argentina, in particular) employ relatively advanced and efficient devices, most production in developing nations continues to utilize the earth and pit kilns considered primitive and inefficient by most analysts of this sector. Donors, acknowledging this problem, have tended to see it as cost-dominated, with improved kilns not being accepted because charcoal makers cannot afford them. The donors have devoted new study to the relative costs and benefits of various production techniques, in order to explore possible ways to overcome these financial hurdles.[26]

However, as a few more perceptive analysts have observed, the poor results of the past have been caused not by mere economic ignorance, but by a more fundamental flaw in the assistance agencies' approach to technical change in this field. Bina Agarwal writes, 'Most studies dealing with charcoal production have devoted space essentially to the technical characteristics of the hardware in use, and to the relative efficiencies of different conversion processes; few have described the socio-economic characteristics of the people making charcoal.'[27] Work to date had been dominated by the assumption that, once the technical problems of carbonization were well understood and designs optimized, conservation of fuelwood resources in the field would follow automatically. Foley comments, 'The focus in many past programmes has been unduly technical. They have attempted to increase the yield, quality and consistency of charcoal making without attempting to discover whether these objectives are relevant to local needs and priorities.'[28] Clearly, the minimal nature of the adoption of new carbonization techniques demonstrates that demand in the charcoal production area is neither well understood nor satisfied by most technology development programmes.

*Lack of knowledge of existing production systems*
A comprehension of the existing users' production systems is a prerequisite for an accurate appreciation of user capabilities and demand in the area of charcoal production. Both the size and the skill-levels of production operations vary enormously between and within developing nations. Some charcoal, especially that destined for large urban markets, is produced by large-scale enterprises, while other supplies originate from individual producers working on a small, irregular basis in this industry. In the former operation, the production process involves numerous participants in addition to those engaged in wood-charcoal conversion, including super-

visors, distributors, sales agents, and transporters, all of whom have particular and interactive needs. Even in the latter situation producer needs can vary greatly depending on sources of fuelwood, and size and location of markets for charcoal produced.

In all cases, the thermodynamic efficiency of production itself can vary enormously in relation to user (producer) situations. Although they may employ the same basic earth or pit kiln technologies, well-organized and monitored operations can achieve much higher charcoal outputs per unit fuelwood inputs than less well structured charcoaling. People making charcoal as a permanent business have different means and objectives from those seeking to supplement their income by salvaging forest materials during spare time from other agricultural practices, and it should be expected that the technologies they develop and manage should differ correspondingly.[29] Moreover, the capabilities of the technology users in these different types of production situations, and their aspirations for technical change, also will differ. Yet, much of past work on charcoal production has treated kiln designs as if they can contribute equally to all situations, as long as they meet certain technical criteria.

*How inefficient are earth and pit kilns?*

There is some concern that the general technical assumptions about the conversion efficiencies of widely used earth and pit kilns may not be completely sound, especially in consideration of the wide variety of production situations and scales in which these are used in developing nations. The literature tends to depict these types of kilns as small in size (less than 20 cubic metres in volume) and crudely constructed, but this is not always the case. In Somalia, for instance, producers erect large earth mound kilns over 100 cubic metres in volume, and even use metal sheets to cover the fuelwood feedstock to minimize earth contamination of the charcoal produced.[30] Moreover, some production operations are run by families that have been in the charcoaling trade for generations, whose members have developed skills in constructing and operating these 'primitive' kilns that enable them to gain consistently higher quality and quantity output than do occasional or less experienced charcoal makers. It seems unlikely that one eficiency rating can categorize the actual performance of the wide range of earth and pit kilns employed in the field in developing countries.

It also appears that what efficiency assumptions have been made are not based on extensive field measurements of kiln performance. Powell's study of charcoal production in Ghana is often cited for its assessment of 5–15 per cent efficiency for traditional earth kilns, compared to the 25 per cent possible in improved models.[31] Yet, it is not clear that his tests were carried out under typical production conditions, using traditional producers. Even the efficiency results of more rarified test conditions can be ambiguous because of problems in measuring the actual input:output energy involved.[32]

The Energy Studies Unit in Malawi conducted a trial of traditional earth kilns and new metal kiln designs, using a traditional charcoal maker to construct and operate the former. They found a 21.5 per cent (by weight) efficiency for the traditional kiln, and 24.2 per cent efficiency for the 'improved' metal design. Their conclusion: 'This is hardly the kind of difference that in itself would warrant a massive conversion to modern charcoal technologies.'[33] A recent review of the literature on charcoal production concluded

> There are few reliable and consistent statistics on the yields obtained using different charcoal making methods. The majority of reports are based on small numbers of trials and cannot be taken as truly representative. . . . Even from the available information, however, it is clear that no matter what charcoal making method is used there are large variations in the yields obtained. A great deal depends on the type of wood used, its moisture content, the weather conditions during charcoal making, and above all the skill of the operator. The result is that there is a substantial degree of overlap between the yields obtained with different manufacturing methods.[34]

There is a far greater problem than one of measurement in these assessments of kiln performance. This problem is the failure of most assessments to understand that 'efficiency' for charcoal makers, the technology users, involves far more than thermodynamic conversion relationships. Efficiency, for the kiln user, often is determined primarily by the *profitability* of his production operation. Profitability, moreover, is generally determined by short term cash flow analyses. A charcoal producer looks at what he pays to construct his kilns and carbonize wood over a season, and how much he earns from his product over that season. If he has to substantially increase his investment to adopt a new kiln, but he does not increase his production or his sales revenues in excess of this increase within the first season of operation, he does not view the technology as 'efficient'. Treating efficiency as a purely physical parameter provides an incomplete and often dangerously misleading basis upon which to design and evaluate new charcoal production devices. Thermodynamic conversion relations are a part of efficiency, but so are economic considerations.

*Wider political economy considerations*
The more thoughtful analyses of the problems in attaining innovation in charcoal production also note that the major obstacles to technical change often lie far beyond the boundaries of physical and economic production parameters. Foley writes,

> whatever the manufacturing methods, one of the dominant features of charcoal making is that there is little effective control over the public lands and reserved forest areas from which the majority of the wood supplies are drawn. . . . The lack of adequate control over the exploitation of wood resources is one of the reasons why charcoal making tends

to have such damaging environmental consequences. ... The fact that most of the wood used for charcoal making is obtained at zero or near zero financial cost also means that there is little incentive for charcoal makers to invest in methods of economising in its use.[35]

Charcoal production should be seen as a part of a larger land management system. Unless that system contains a need to maximize the utility and sustained supply of its forest resource, it is difficult to see much potential for change in conversion efficiency, regardless of the technical prowess of whatever kiln designs are invented. Work in charcoal production technology should, therefore, look to what land management concerns do exist to find the needs to support the innovations it wishes to bring about, promoting charcoal production as a part of larger improved land utilization efforts.

## 2. Improved wood-burning stoves

Projects to improve household wood-burning (i.e., wood or charcoal) stoves have existed since the 1940s, when stove programmes were started in India.[36] As in the area of charcoal production, the focus of most work in this area has been on technical improvements to the wood fuel combustion system, as it is clear that thermodynamic improvements on the combustion efficiency of typical open fires are possible, in the sense that designs produced and tested in laboratories can achieve far higher efficiencies than 3-stone fires tested under those same circumstances.

Improved stove work has enjoyed substantial attention and priority in development assistance, particularly since the first petroleum crisis of 1973.[37] As a result, the literature on new stove designs and the documentation of their production in numerous countries has grown enormously, and, like in the area of charcoal production, the hardware-oriented, insular R & D approach of the field has become more and more entrenched. Considerable funds have been allocated for the construction and equipping of laboratories devoted solely to stove design development and testing.

However, some field workers involved in stoves programmes have questioned the effectiveness of this technology-driven strategy.[38] Donor assistance policy in the stoves area has been influenced by the articulation of much of this field observation in a critical review of stoves activity published by the Earthscan organization in 1983. The review noted that most stove programmes failed to live up to their planners' expectations in getting improved stoves into large numbers of households. Moreover, the study claimed that most stoves that were adopted achieved little of their promised energy savings in practice.[39]

The Earthscan report caused a great deal of controversy at the time of its release, but subsequent developments in the stoves field show that its claims are being acknowledged. As in the case of charcoal production work, the failure to recognize and address user demand resulted in many designs being unacceptable to the people they sought to benefit.[40]

43

*Stove dissemination*

One of the political effects of this critical analysis of the shortcomings of stove improvement programmes has been an increase in donor interest in the extra-R & D aspects of project implementation. A conference on wood stove dissemination, involving representatives from 17 nations and sponsored by five national donor agencies, was held in the Netherlands from 31 October to 10 November 1983.[41] K Krishna Prasad, one of the organizers of the conference, and the director of a major stove R & D laboratory at Eindehoven, noted in his preface to the proceedings of the meeting,

> General opinion now considers that the dissemination process will be a critical factor in the technology reaching the population concerned. . . . More detailed information, particularly on the dissemination process and its linkage to the R & D system, is urgently needed for significant progress in stoves projects implementation to be made.[42]

While this movement away from a laboratory focus is encouraging, it is not certain that the new embrace of 'dissemination' as a key issue provides a key to achieving innovation in the stoves sector. One of the major problems with this new intellectual trend is the uncertain meaning given 'dissemination' by those who expound upon its importance. In the conference proceedings, essays by Prasad, Ki-Zerbo, and most of the case study authors regard dissemination as an issue of information, much in the manner of the treatment of 'diffusion' by Rogers, criticized in the previous chapter.[43] The dissemination problem is treated simply as a problem of how to get a fixed design adopted, or, in Prasad's case, how to get designers enough information so that their labs can come up with the proper designs in the first place. Much attention is devoted to how government and non-government organizations can gain public attention and enlist public involvement in spreading the designs the organizations have invented around.

However, the issue facing stove programmes is not one of information, but of how to enlist greater user participation in innovation. This entails more than questions of how to raise public awareness. Some of the participants in the conference recognize these different, more complex issues underlying stove dissemination problems. Massé writes,

> When stove programmes begin, they are almost immediately supplied with offices, showrooms, workshops, bricklayer teams, foreign experts, cars, and international finance. In this way, they ignore all the existing informal circuits of the environment to which they are supposed to be introducing technical innovation.[44]

He implies that the user role in innovation begins not after technology design, but as a part of this process, and that, by insulating technology formation behind a barrier of external capital and 'expertise', the probability of achieving successful innovation is diminished.

Ashok Khosla, one of the three entrepreneurs present at this conference on dissemination, adds that manufacturers and distributors of stoves should also be considered in this early design stage:

> the innovation process must link the design of the technologies much more closely to the needs of manufacturing and marketing than has generally been done in the past. No matter how efficient a design may be in laboratory tests, or how well it is claimed to fulfil socio-economic criteria, it cannot be considered complete or acceptable until methods of producing it have been worked out, and it is field tested. ... the design of an appropriate technology, no less than that of a new electronics product or automobile model, must be carried out within the framework of an organization which also has responsibilities for manufacturing and marketing. If this is not the case, market success will be only a matter of pure chance.[45]

Khosla points out that producers and distributors were also technology users, whose needs should be accommodated in order to achieve successful technical change.

Maxwell Kinyanjui's description of the Kenyan *jiko* stoves programme contrasts sharply from the other case studies in its reliance on existing formal and informal sector commercial operations for stove production and distribution.[46] The Kenyan programme relies extensively on traditional stove-making artisans, adapting improved stove designs to fit their needs and capabilities. It acknowledges that the traditional production and sales system is skilful and well organized, and works with, not outside, that system to develop its improved jiko design. The Kenyan example, in which an expanding and self-sustaining improved stove production and sales programme has resulted, supports Khosla's contention that accommodating producer and distributor needs in the design process is an important part of successful innovation.

*Stove dissemination studies: a step in the right direction*
Although it has its shortcomings, the new attention given dissemination issues represents an important step from a technology-driven, relatively unsuccessful improved stoves policy, towards a more needs-oriented, and hopefully more successful new stance. The inclusion of a marketing specialist among the participants and the Netherlands conference shows particular promise, because market research, as has been discussed in relation to the health and development field, can contribute much towards the identification of user needs and capabilities.[47]

However, producing pamphlets and pictures to enhance public awareness of stoves efforts is not a sufficient means of achieving successful innovation. Stove programmes will repeat past mistakes unless stove 'experts' develop ways to receive ideas from technology users, and not only means for dictating fixed designs to them. The experts should concentrate on developing a mechanism for incorporating user inputs into the R & D system itself.

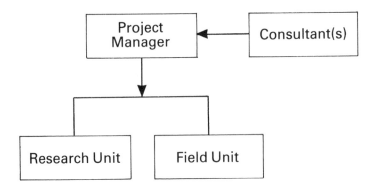

EARLY ORGANIZATIONAL STRUCTURE

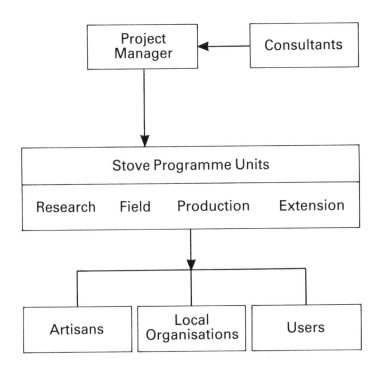

LATER ORGANIZATIONAL STRUCTURE

Figure 3.1 *R & D organization charts*

The limited attention paid to this user-R & D interaction in present stove improvement work is shown in the R & D organization charts shown in Figure 3.1 above, presented by the Intermediate Technology Development Group as an example of possible institutional structures for stove programmes.[48] The bottom structure may be an improvement on the original research organization, but it does not represent the sort of interactive research that is generating innovation in agriculture, health, and irrigation (as described in the preceding chapter). These organization charts need to present their arrows pointing in both directions, not only from 'experts' to users.

Education and information dissemination are essential ingredients in securing technology adoption, but user participation is equally important. Stove programmes need to channel information and skills *from* technology users into the design process, bringing users into the R & D system itself. As Bina Agarwal aptly remarks,

> The most significant pointer provided by the review of the diffusion literature relating to attempts to promote improved improved wood-burning stoves, is the importance of adapting the stove to the users' needs and *of involving the potential beneficiaries as closely as possible in the designing and building of the stoves* [emphasis mine].[49]

The available literature indicates that stove programmes need a dissemination focus to make up for previous lack of attention to the specific needs of consumers, producers, and distributors that has contributed to the disappointing results of many past efforts; but they also need a comprehensive innovation management strategy that permits these needs to become a more active part of technology development, through providing for greater technology user involvement in this process.

## 3. Forestry

Forestry as a development assistance field has a longer pedigree than either charcoal production or improved wood-burning stoves, but forestry's relationship with energy concerns, from the donors' standpoint, began after the petroleum price increases and the rise of energy as a separate discipline in the 1970s. The rise of fuelwood production as an important goal of forestry contributed to a development of new forms of forestry itself, in both its technical and administrative aspects. New species of little use for timber or other wood products, but fast growing and (in some cases) drought tolerant, became the subject of research and field trials. New planting methods and patterns far different from traditional block plantations and reserves were investigated.Integrating tree growing into agricultural situations became the focus of the new discipline of agroforestry.[50]

Projects were implemented to undertake afforestation, with fuelwood as a prime object of production, not only at the large plantation level, but also in community and individual farm situations. The management of such smaller level schemes raised a host of issues foresters had not encountered before, particularly those stemming from the social and economic milieu in which they were working.[51] Social and economic factors often were the source of the greatest obstacles to forestry development under these new conditions.[52]

*Evaluation of 'new' forestry performance*
Since 1984, major forestry donor agencies, such as FAO and USAID, have been undertaking an extensive review of their new forestry activities, to observe how well they have fared under the new social and economic conditions in which they operated. These evaluations have concluded that, while some good results have occurred in the more humid tropics, arid and semi-arid zone forestry has seen little progress. The FAO commented in a background paper to its expert consultation on the role of forestry in combatting desertification, 'While considerable progress has been made in agricultural, forestry, livestock, industrial and tourism development in the wetter zones, little has been done so far for the low rainfall areas.'[53] USAID's own submission to this meeting echoed this assessment in its appraisal of forestry work in the Sahelian zone of Africa, which by 1985, in spite of some 200 million dollars from multi-donor forestry assistance, faced again the havoc created by a new drought.[54]

Fred Weber, a forester involved in work in the Sahel for the last 20 years, expressed the following sober assessment of progress in the field at a USAID Africa Forestry review meeting in 1984: 'More accurate information still lacking, I have the very worrisome feeling that even today four out of five trees leaving the nurseries are dead by the time they should be one year old.'[55] He also noted that, even in cases where fuelwood had been produced and made available, difficulties had been encountered in selling it: 'The apparent paradox of the firewood crisis and large stacks of firewood cut from plantations still waiting for buyers only shows that many factors are at play which lie beyond the reach of simplistic money market economics,' he concluded.[56]

Perhaps the consummate example of failure in the new fuelwood forestry was provided by a USAID fuelwood plantation project in the Gambia. This project cleared 600 hectares of natural forest in order to restock it with fast-growing, more productive *Gmelina* species. However, four years after clear-felling, the Forest Department had succeeded only in replanting 60 hectares, so that overall a huge loss of fuelwood and other forest resources had occurred.[57] The project was contributing to deforestation, rather than afforestation.

The Gambia episode might seem ludicrous, but it is unlikely that it is unique. Even forestry projects that have received high praise for their physical outputs have come in for criticism that they are not providing the benefits they promised. India's social forestry programmes in Gujarat and Karnataka, for example, have come under attack by local sources who complained that the *Eucalyptus* species cultivated did not serve the needs of the poor (for forage and soil improvement as well as fuel), but rather the needs of wealthier pulp and poles suppliers.[58] Moreover, it was argued, the poorest communities, that could benefit the most from afforestation activities, were passed over by the programme in favour of less remote, better off villages.[59] Even the World Bank's own evaluation of the Gujarat project, while largely favorable, expressed concern over 'the extent to which the project will benefit the landless.'[60]

Faced with the poor progress of much of its effort to improve and increase forest resources in arid and semi-arid regions, the donors have begun to reassess their approach to forestry itself. It appears they have decided that this approach, like that for other forest energy technologies described earlier, was too technology-centred and would profit from user need inputs. They also have begun to move, on paper at least, towards a transformation in the institutional stance of forestry itself, so that it could better receive these inputs.

*Towards a more user-involved innovation strategy*
The documentation that has emerged from recent donor forestry meetings, such as those cited previously, calls for forestry to move away from a 'sectoral' focus towards a more 'integrated' approach. This terminology means essentially that forestry should move from an isolated, wood production-oriented posture, towards a role as a part of larger rural development efforts. The FAO points out that its old stance might be appropriate for temperate regions, but not for the environments of most developing nations:

> Forestry practice imported from temperate regions was developed in countries with more or less settled land tenure and land use and where more or less clear distinctions are possible as to what constitutes forestry, agricultural or grazing land situation not prevailing in arid and semi-arid regions.[61]

The suggested integrated approach contains two essential institutional innovations: making forestry an element of greater land management objectives, rather than an end in itself; and making forestry departments into service-(as opposed to enforcement-)oriented institutions.

In the former area, forestry and foresters have to move from an emphasis on establishing forest stands and meeting production targets, to one on forestry's contribution in larger efforts to improve food and animal production conditions, conserve the environment (and, in particular, water resources), and provide rural employment and income-generating opportunities.[62] Just as desertification and deforestation are not merely fuelwood problems, neither can their solutions depend solely on either the techniques or the contributions of foresters. As USAID's forestry advisors note,

49

Even the limited experience to-date has shown that rural people have seldom been enthusiastic about planting trees specifically and uniquely to produce fuelwood. This narrowly defined objective has tended to be rather self-limiting and has understated the real value of trees to rural people. *An exclusively 'fuelwood approach' actually exacerbates the dichotomy between agriculture and forestry* [emphasis theirs] by reinforcing the ill-conceived notion that somehow the foresters alone are going to resolve the fuelwood/environment problem.[63]

They recommend that forestry institutions concentrate on measures through which tree planting can enhance agricultural productivity, and that they modify their extension systems to create multidisciplinary services that can accommodate not only forestry, but also agricultural and livestock needs.[64] The FAO, too, urges that forestry training provide for greater understanding of agricultural, animal, and environmental concerns.[65]

The other innovation required for forestry institutions is to turn them from isolated operators occupied with protecting their territories into interactive organizations aimed at working with others to achieve the higher objectives described above. As the FAO comments, 'It will be necessary to substitute "servicing" and developmental activities for the restrictive measures and police activities of the past.'[66] This service role has to be one ruled not by forest utilization regulations and their law enforcement considerations, but by a commitment to a two-way exchange of opinions, knowledge, and ideas between foresters and rural people. The FAO points out that this implies some different considerations for national forest policies:

– Wood production *per se* need not be the primary objective in the drier parts of arid zones, except as a by-product of shelterbelt or soil stabilization measures;
– The dependence of man and his livestock on these lands needs to be recognized as a *de facto* component of the environment; policy should therefore aim at reconciling and harmonizing this requirement with the overall management rather than treating it under the category of 'forest enemies' to be suppressed or eliminated.[67]

The development of a service-oriented forestry of necessity will entail the corresponding development of greater user involvement in forestry technology innovation, as the semantic progression of FAO's depiction of its own forestry duly confirms. In 1978, inspired by the popular forestry focus of the 8th World Forestry Congress in Jakarta, the FAO launched its 'Forestry for Local Community Development' programme.[68] This programme brought fuelwood into a greater prominence in forestry activities; but, to a large extent it still considered forestry a separate activity from other rural functions. It was an activity that was the domain of trained foresters, focusing on village woodlots and similar segregated forestry measures more than on integrated, agroforestry options. By 1981, however, the FAO was writing about 'Forestry for Rural Development', a title which signified a greater interest in rural agricultural and other needs, and how these could be satisfied through foresters' activities.[69] In 1985 the FAO completed the semantic incorporation of rural people into forestry technology development in its latest report, 'Tree Growing By Rural People'.[70] Now it was the rural people – the technology users – rather than forestry professionals, who were the focus of the development programme.

In suggesting a movement towards a greater integration with rural agricultural and other land use management objectives, and the adoption of a more service-orientated posture, the donors are placing forestry work in a position where it can more easily receive and respond to user inputs to its technology development process. Their more technology-driven, institutionally-introverted earlier efforts were not successful, for the most part, in dealing with the social and economic constraints facing forestry development by and for rural people and rural communities. The new approach they are suggesting represents an innovation strategy that will stress the user role both in the design and the implementation of forestry projects, and, if the experience in other development areas is valid in this case, this approach should find greater success in changing the forest resource base in arid and semi-arid regions.

## Users, R & D, and renewable energy

In both the renewable energy field as a whole, and in the particular forest energy technologies examined, much of the work of the past ten years of development assistance has been dominated by the attitude that, if energy could be produced through an initial installation of technologies by experts, its benefits would soon flow to large populations. As the donors have acknowledged, the benefits of these technologies, for the most part, are not being realized, largely because the development process itself has not been responsive to the demands of the beneficiaries. Moreover, the significant potential of these beneficiaries, the intended eventual users of the technologies, to assist in this development process largely has not been utilized. There now seems to be a growing recognition that more demand-responsive, user-involved innovation strategies should be pursued.

The renewable energy field, therefore, is just beginning to explore an innovation strategy entered into earlier by other development disciplines, as well as by industrial strategists in developed nations. There is every reason to believe that this more participation-oriented technology development strategy will bring better results than the previous technology-driven approach. The analysis of specific technology development in charcoal production, improved charcoal stoves, and forestry in Sudan shows the actual benefits of user participation for renewable energy innovation.

# CHAPTER FOUR
## Sudan and the Sudan Renewable Energy Project

Sudan, like many other developing countries, relies extensively on forest energy resources for its national energy needs. Its total energy consumption in 1980 was estimated at 7 million tonnes oil equivalent (toe), of which over 5.9 million toe (approximately 85 per cent) was in the form of wood, charcoal, or agricultural residues consumption.[1] Household energy use accounted for 83 per cent of total energy consumption. This is despite an almost 50 per cent increase in the use of petroleum products between 1970 and 1980.

Sudan's reliance on its biomass resource base for much of its energy needs is typical for many developing nations. Its poor knowledge of the present state of this resource, and of production/consumption effects on future supplies, is also typical. There has never been a national forest inventory. Present forest resource figures are based on estimates made during the 1950s and 1960s, without the benefits of aerial reconnaissance techniques. A recent attempt to upgrade this information through a review of 1972 Landsat imagery revised growing stock estimates down from 32 to only 8 cubic metres per year.[2] The study also concluded that, at present rates of consumption versus regeneration and afforestation, all forested areas in northern Sudan would be denuded within 20 years.[3] Later studies have postulated that Sudan's and other Sahelian nations' forests are now in a state of accelerating depletion, with deforestation rates increasing as the resource base diminishes.[4]

The forest resource is unevenly distributed, so that some regions of Sudan consume far less than is produced each year, while others consume far more than is produced. Firewood and charcoal are transported as much as 600 kilometres from the Blue Nile, Upper Nile, and Southern Kordofan provinces (and perhaps also from across the Ethiopian border), to markets in Khartoum province. Forest resources in the Blue Nile and southern Kassala provinces make similar voyages hundreds of kilometres eastwards to Kassala town and to Port Sudan on the Red Sea. The area around Juba, a large and growing town in southern Sudan, is becoming heavily deforested, while vast forest resources within 100–200 kilometres lie unexploited due to the absence of roads and transport to reach them.

Although the biomass resource sector is not well researched and monitored by government, it has been closely watched for some time by local wood products producers and traders. Charcoal making is big and long-established business in central Sudan. It is also a major source of dry

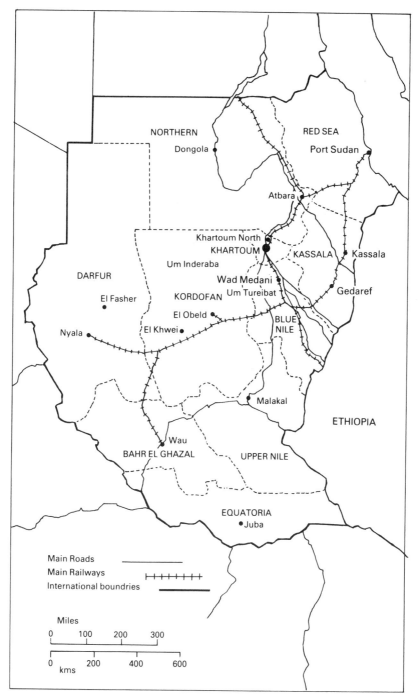

Figure 4.1 *Sudan*

season migrant employment in the central and eastern regions.[5] The production and sale of charcoal stoves is a significant source of informal employment in urban areas. The distribution of firewood, charcoal, and other forest products such as poles and matting is another profitable enterprise.[6]

As resources have declined, forest product prices have increased. A sack (100 lbs, approximately) of charcoal that cost Ls4 in late 1982 sold for Ls17 in January 1987.[7] Sales of firewood, poles, and charcoal have begun in places where formerly all forest products were freely gathered from nearby. The higher prices have made forest energy consumers very sensitive to market fuel quality, and to fuel conservation potential.

## Government – Professionalism, Decentralization, and the Forest Resource

Two characteristics of the Sudanese human resource are of particular significance to work concerning the forest resource and forest energy development. The first is the higher amount of university degree holders (BA, BSc, or higher) per unit population than for neighbouring African nations. According to UNESCO statistics, displayed in Table 4.1 below, Sudan leads all its neighbours by a large margin, with the exception of Egypt, whose development has been more tied to Middle Eastern than to African politics and economics. Although UNESCO does not prepare separate statistics on the educational backgrounds of civil service staffs, the dominance of government positions as employment of first resource in all African nations makes it likely that the Government of Sudan possesses a

**Table 4.1 Students in university (third level) education per 100,000 population**

| Country | Year | Number |
|---|---|---|
| Sudan | 1981 | 246 |
| Zimbabwe | 1983 | 219 |
| Kenya | 1983 | 75 |
| Egypt | 1982 | 1902 |
| Burkina Faso | 1983 | 81 |
| Ethiopa | 1983 | 83 |
| Mali | 1982 | 143 |
| Niger | 1983 | 67 |
| Uganda | 1982 | 76 |
| Botswana | 1983 | 167 |
| Tanzania | 1981 | 54 |

*Source:* UNESCO Statistical Yearbook, 1985.

correspondingly high percentage of university graduates within its various departments.

The second factor distinguishing Sudan from its neighbours is the higher number of science graduates it produces. While Kenya trained only eight engineers in 1982, and Mali only 714, Sudan reported 2418 students in engineering courses at the university or polytechnic level.[8] Also of particular concern to forest energy technology development, Sudan has maintained at least 150 professional and technical forest staff in its civil service since it became independent in 1956.[9] This far exceeds most, if not all, other African national forester resources.

The Government of Sudan gives special prominence to science, and particularly to research, in the civil service. The head of the National Council for Research until very recently possessed ministerial status, a ranking rarely offered corresponding officials in developed country governments.[10] There is a reverence for academic achievement in general among political authorities, so that, as in many other nations, elder, traditional leaders often will defer to the presence and opinions of a far younger Masters or Ph.D. degree engineer or scientist, even if the latter has little work experience.

The high representation of academically trained personnel in the civil service, and the high respect for science within that service and within the national politics and culture, constitute both an asset and a liability for technology development activities. They are an asset in that they, in theory, provide a greater capacity to pursue technical change within government institutions. They are a potential liability in that the exalted position given technical staff can easily be transformed into an isolated position, one in which their status serves as a barrier to potentially constructive interaction with people and knowledge found outside of the formal R & D system.

*Decentralization*

Sudan possesses extensive central and regional government organizations, but until recently regional government power was significant only in the southern region.[11] In 1971 the Local Government Act channelled most central ministry activities through People's Province Executive Councils, creating, in theory, a joint decision-making system. In 1980 the Regional Government Act divided the north into 5 regions, establishing full regional financial and legal authority over many aspects of government. The Act sought to improve the potential of local administrations, which had been in existence since the colonial period. Considering the size of Sudan and its poor transport facilities, decentralized government seemed a reasonable proposition.

However, decentralization produced great confusion and disruption in the forestry sector. The 1980 legislation sought to leave natural resource management under central control, but at the same time it drastically

55

curbed the authority of the Central Ministry of Agriculture, and its Central Forestry Administration. The regional forestry departments and their staff came under regional government control, so that, although the forest reserves in the region remained technically under central governance, in practice they became the property of local government.

When it became apparent that the regions would not receive development funds commensurate with their new staffs, authority, and obligations, they began to investigate means by which their local resources could compensate for this. Regions with substantial forest reserves soon found that royalties for land clearance, charcoal production, and other forest product rights provided good revenue opportunities. The financially weak local governments were not concerned with the longer term natural resource supply and demand situation, nor with managing forest exploitation on a sensible and sustainable basis. From 1971 to 1985 a sizeable portion of forest reserves in the Eastern, Central, and Kordofan regions were cut while little new planting was undertaken. Moreover, revenues from royalties were not utilized to maintain forestry department staff and equipment, so what little ability existed for local resource management was eroded.

One of the first acts of the present government's Minister of Agriculture and its ministerial level Natural Resources Committee was the re-centralization of agricultural and forestry sector responsibilities.[12] The consequences of this decision, taken in late 1985, are not yet clear.


## Government Institutions in the Energy Sector

The Government of Sudan, like most other governments, created organizations with energy sector responsibility only recently. The Ministry of Energy and Mining (MEM) was established in 1977, incorporating a number of units with energy responsibilities that had been distributed among various ministries and other government departments.[13] The assignment and co-ordination of responsibilities, particularly in the traditional and renewable energy areas, remains far from complete.


*Government ministries*

The Ministry of Energy and Mining contains three organizations with direct energy responsibility, and a fourth with indirect responsibility (see Figure 4.2 below). The General Petroleum Corporation (GPC) and National Electricity Corporation (NEC) are statutory bodies under the control of the Minister. The National Energy Administration (NEA) was formed in 1980, with financial assistance from USAID, to handle energy planning and assessment tasks. It is a part of the Ministry itself, and the Director of NEA reports to the Undersecretary. The National Water Corporation (NWC), another part of the Ministry, plays an important

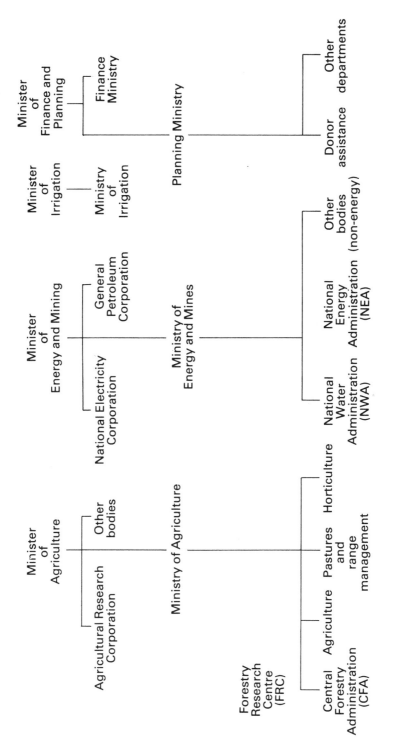

Figure 4.2 *Government of Sudan Ministerial organizations with energy responsibilities*

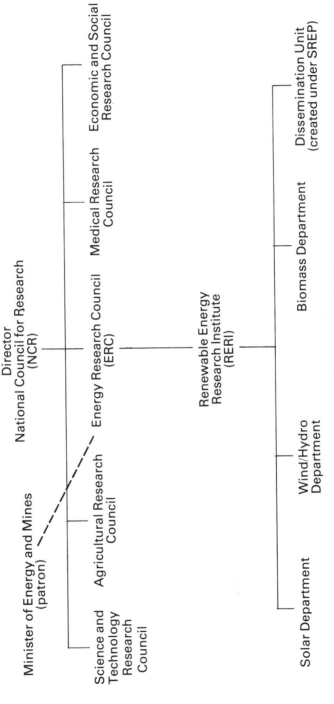

Figure 4.3 *Government of Sudan Research and Development organizations*

energy role because of the significant amount of fuel required for irrigation and drinking water delivery in many parts of the country.

The Ministries of Agriculture and Irrigation also are involved in energy matters, through their resource production and conservation responsibilities. The Ministry of Agriculture contains the Central Forestry Administration (CFA), which is made up of the Afforestation, Inventory and Management, Utilization, Gum Arabic, and Administration and Finance sections. There is also a system of regional Forestry Departments, which are responsible to regional Ministries of Natural Resources.

*Research institutions and universities*
Government research institutions and universities also play a major role in the energy sector, particularly in the renewable energy field. The University of Khartoum has carried out experimentation in renewable energy technologies, primarily solar thermal technologies (distillation, drying, water heating, solar architecture) from soon after independence. The university's agricultural faculty has taken a great interest of late in fuelwood and agricultural residue energy concerns (mostly biogas and briquetting). The new University of Gezira has a general agricultural focus, and has been carrying out experimentation on photovoltaic pumping systems.

The Government's co-ordinating body for all R & D activities, the National Council for Research (NCR), was founded in 1967 (its administrative departments and structure are shown in Figure 4.3, above).[14] Institutional energy R & D began in 1970 under the NCR's Science and Technology Research Council. This council supported the creation of the Institute of Related and Environmental Studies, within the Engineering Faculty of the University of Khartoum, to provide laboratory space for energy research. In 1973 this institute changed its name to the Solar Energy Research Institute, and in 1975 it again changed this title to the Energy Research Institute, and moved its headquarters to a new building owned by the NCR.

The NCR Director formed a new organization, the Energy Research Council (ERC), in 1980, and transferred the Energy Research Institute from the Science and Technology Research Council to the control of this new institution, which became the fifth of the NCR's councils. As a council, it was not itself an institute, with a large staff of researchers, but a co-ordinating board to oversee and shape the operations of the Energy Research Institute, consisting of representatives from all government organizations involved in energy work. The Energy Research Institute was renamed the Renewable Energy Research Institute (RERI) in 1983 to reflect its focus on alternative energy resources.

RERI in 1982 consisted of three sections: Solar, Wind/Hydro, and Biomass. All three were headed by recent graduates, two Ph.D. and one M.Sc engineers. The RERI director and ERC director were both Ph.D.'s. The institute staff consisted entirely of technical and clerical personnel, with no economic or social science disciplines represented. It was a young, highly acredited, technically focused body with little practical experience.[25] As a result, RERI's inclination was towards the implementation of design and testing programmes within the confines of its laboratory facilities at the University of Khartoum, and its field station at Soba.

## The Sudan Renewable Energy Project

It is common for several years to pass between the initial conceptualization of an aid project and its initial implementation steps. This was the case for the Government of Sudan and USAID's Sudan Renewable Energy Project (SREP), which began as the 'Rural Renewable Energy Project' in a consultancy report in early 1980, but which did not begin implementation until October 1982.[15] The delay had a profound effect on SREP, because it moved its initiation into a new period in USAID Africa Bureau thinking about the implementation of energy projects. While the concept paper and early project design work were firmly grounded in the 'design and demonstration' practices of the 1970s, the intervening period saw a change in attitude about the project. Emphasis came more on the extent of technology introduction and use, as opposed to the quality of in-house research and testing.

The Georgia Institute of Technology (GIT), the contractor awarded the implementation of SREP, recognized this new USAID attitude in its technical proposal for SREP implementation.[16] GIT emphasized the importance of getting technologies to be produced and adopted in quantity, and distributed over a wide geographic area. The project contained two central tasks: 'commercializing' suitable renewable energy technologies, and developing the RERI as an institution to play a key role in this process. It was also agreed that the project need not focus exclusively on work in rural areas, but could cover technologies that affect rural resource development, such as improved charcoal stoves that reduce forest resource demand. This agreement led to the retitling of the project from the 'rural renewable energy project' to the Sudan Renewable Energy Project.

The USAID project managers urged that its work focus upon attracting technology producers and users to renewable energy activities, and that it should avoid excessive reliance on 'research', which was seen as a secluded, academic process, with few short-term results.[17] SREP, from this initial conception, was to be a project that escaped the failures of previous 'demonstration projects' that had come in for much US Government criticism.

SREP contained two principal elements designed to facilitate the attainment of commercialization: support for institutional development of innovation capability, and a financial incentive for the creation of greater ERC links to technology users outside of its institutional confines. The lines of authority and support contained in the project are depicted in Figure 4.4, below.

# MANPOWER

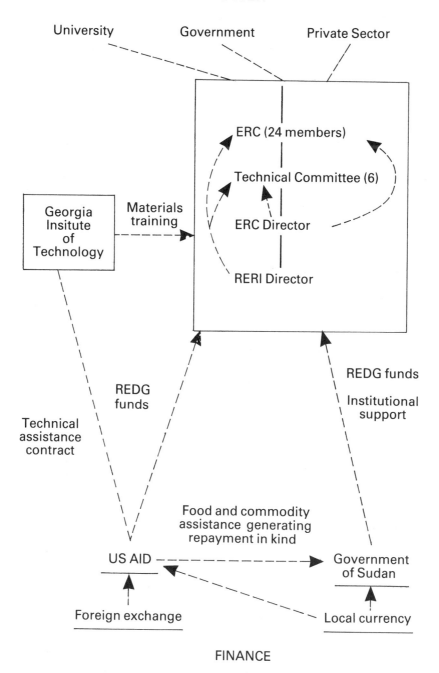

Figure 4.4 *Lines of authority and support in SREP*

## Institutional development

Under SREP, the RERI received institutional support to create new divisions devoted to economic and social evaluation, and dissemination of renewable energy technologies. USAID provided funds for training and procurement of materials and equipment, and the Government of Sudan, using local currency provided as part of its bilateral development programme with USAID, increased RERI staff to meet the new assignments. A concurrent West German (GTZ) assistance project was to provide a new RERI headquarters building, but this construction was delayed and, by October 1985, was not underway.

During SREP's implementation, the ERC decided that institutional needs would best be served by the creation of one new department, the Dissemination Unit, which would form RERI's fourth section. This unit would be responsible for technical evaluation and production development, economic and social evaluation, and educational and promotional activities. New staff were hired, including economists, home economists, engineers, journalists, artists, and foresters.[18]

## Renewable Energy Development Grants

The second important contribution of SREP was the formation of a Renewable Energy Development Grants (REDG) programme. This programme contained both dollar and local currency funds, which were to be used to help initiate renewable energy activities that would then become self-sustaining. Approximately $3 million in dollars and Sudanese pounds (at 1981 equivalencies) was provided for the REDG programme, roughly 60 per cent of the entire SREP budget.[19] Most important was the caveat, imposed by USAID, that REDG funds could only be disbursed to parties and activities *outside* the ERC's own R & D system.[20]

The ERC and its contractor technical advisor, GIT, were asked to develop a system for grant selection, disbursement, monitoring and evaluation. The resulting programme centered upon a six-person Technical Committee, made up of ERC members selected by the full council, that received and evaluated all grant proposals, with approved applications sent on to the USAID Project Manager for concurrence. The Technical Committee was assisted in its deliberations by a grant review process, involving Sudanese experts in the relevant technical and economic fields. Each application received by the ERC director, who served as the administrator of the Technical Committee, was assigned to at least two reviewers, whose reports were submitted to all committee members in advance of their grants review meeting.

The two central elements of SREP provided a motivation for the pursuit of a user-interactive technology development strategy even before the particular technologies to be developed under SREP had been selected. A regional study had listed 29 renewable energy applications that could be suitable for the project.[21] Yet, USAID and the Government of Sudan did not specify in their project agreement which renewable energy technologies were to be the subject of SREP. Technology selection took place at a meeting in May 1983 between representatives of USAID, ERC, and GIT, as a part of the formulation of the project's initial work plan, while the REDG programme procedures and institutional development plans were established in December 1982.

Thus, SREP contained an *ex ante* commitment to involving the ERC more closely with technology users. Before it was known what technologies would be a part of the project, a central aspect of the way in which those technologies would be developed had been determined. To gain access to the bulk of the finance promised by USAID, the ERC had to strengthen its ties with individuals and organizations outside its own research facilities who could contribute to the design and introduction of the selected technologies.

The May 1983 meeting chose five technologies for SREP: forestry, improved charcoal stoves, improved wood stoves, improved charcoal kilns, and small-scale photovoltaic power applications.[22] The three technologies that received the greatest project attention during the author's three years with SREP were forestry, improved charcoal stoves, and improved charcoal kilns, and technology development in these areas provides the focus of the following chapters.

### REDG programme development

The Technical Committee created temporary advisory committees for each of the technology areas, charged with outlining the types of activities that could be supported by the REDG programme. Once these committees had reported, they were replaced by a single Project Leader for each area, responsible both for soliciting grants applications and for monitoring the progress of each grant awarded. Project Leaders were drawn from RERI staff, where suitable expertise was available. In other cases, such as forestry/fuelwood production, a retired senior forester was hired as a long-term consultant for this position. The two long term GIT technical staff served only as advisors to the system, and did not have a vote in approving or disapproving grant applications.

The ERC Director originally served as the co-ordinator of the entire REDG programme, calling on ERC/SREP clerical assistance when necessary. As the programme grew in size and geographical scope, and other project and donor obligations put greater demands on the Director's time, it was decided to appoint a Grants Administrator. She insured that all new applications were reviewed according to established procedures and timetables, and that all extant grants were monitored on a timely basis. The RERI Dissemination Unit assisted in promoting the REDG programme through publications, workshops, and seminars. Its staff also was involved in monitoring and evaluation tasks.

## Energy, Sudanese Institutions, and SREP

This chapter has introduced several characteristics of the Sudanese physical and socio-political-economic environment that affect forest energy resources and their development. The diversity of the land and its people makes it essential that local resources and demands are considered in any introduction of new technologies. The fragmentation of authority over forestry and energy issues weakens Government influence over individual areas, and increases the importance of local opinions and organizations. The relatively poor understanding of supply and demand for forest energy resources within the Government (and, for that matter, within aid agencies working in Sudan) hinders technology development in this area, and makes the investigation of existing production and consumption a priority for innovation efforts.

In their formulation of SREP, USAID and the Government of Sudan responded to these conditions and constraints, and sought to overcome the latter through the implementation of a user-oriented innovation strategy. The key assumption behind SREP's reliance on the REDG programme was that the grants mechanism, given sufficient institutional support, would attract greater user involvement in technology development efforts, by providing incentives for local producers, distributors, and consumers to design their own energy projects, with technical assistance from ERC staff. In so doing, the grants programme would increase the likelihood of successful innovation in such efforts. The following chapters present the successful results of this exercise in user-interactive technology development.

## CHAPTER FIVE

# Improved Charcoal Production in Sudan

'Improved charcoal production' generally connotes improvements to the kiln system for converting firewood inputs to charcoal product. Indeed, as was discussed in Chapter 3, most technical assistance efforts in the charcoal production area have concentrated on changing established conversion systems. The assumption behind such efforts is that existing technologies are 'inefficient', and that the sooner they are completely replaced by more 'modern' methods, the better for both the production system and forest resource conservation.

Such an assumption is dangerous for two reasons. First, it is often based on a brief, qualitative analysis of existing production systems that does not correctly portray their efficiency. Second, and more important from the standpoint of this dissertation, it promotes a one-directional, non-interactive innovation strategy, as it encourages the idea that the key to change lies in persuading technology users to adopt new kiln designs and methods passed on from the R & D sector. Local skills and knowledge, in this point of view, cannot be of use to innovation.

The Energy Research Council's work on improved charcoal production in Sudan found that local charcoal producers and distributors possessed considerable technical and commercial expertise, and that their production systems obtained high efficiencies, both in physical and economic terms. The ERC's investigations have reversed previously held opinions about the industry and led to the development of an innovation strategy for this technical field that involves not a one-way passage of ideas from R & D down to users, but an interactive technology development strategy in which users play an important and directing role.

## Improved Kiln Design as an Initial SREP Priority

Several factors combined to make charcoal production methods an obvious choice for the group of renewable energy technologies selected for SREP development. The National Energy Assessment, completed by the Ministry of Energy and Mining's National Energy Administration (NEA) in 1983, showed the integral role of charcoal in the energy supply/demand situation. Charcoal use constituted over 27 per cent of total energy consumption in Sudan in 1980.[1] The central part of Sudan, consisting of the Central, Eastern, and Khartoum areas, consumed 43 per cent of the total national output. Including Northern Region consumption, much of which

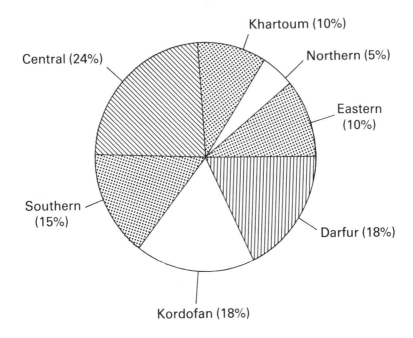

Figure 5.1 *Charcoal consumption by region*

relies on supplies from the central production sites, this area accounts for almost half of total charcoal production in the nation.[2] (see Figure 5.1 above)

Charcoal production's role in overall forest resource demand was even greater. Using previous wood-charcoal conversion estimates, the NEA calculated that charcoal production accounted for 61 per cent of the forest resource consumed through all manners of exploitation (energy, timber products, browse, land clearance for agriculture, etc.) and losses from fires. While twice as much firewood was consumed as charcoal, in energy terms, charcoal consumption entailed the overall utilization of twice the forest resource exploited in firewood consumption.[3]

Much of this charcoal was produced from forest resources in a relatively small part of this central area, with the principal supply sites found in the Blue Nile and Kassala provinces. From these southern sources the charcoal was transported up to 600 kilometres away to northern markets. The

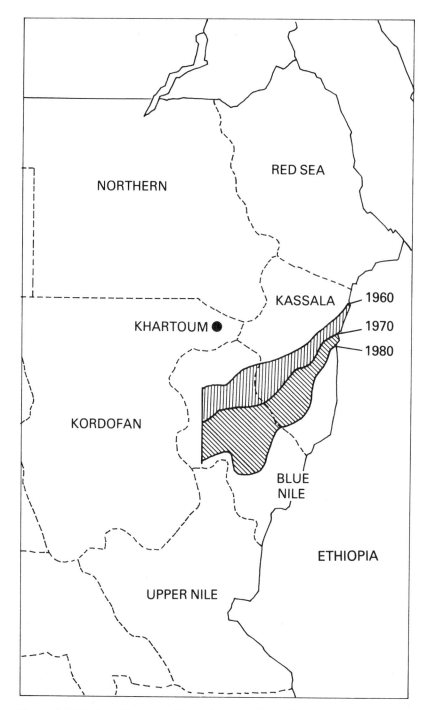

Figure 5.2 *Sudan: Northern limit of charcoal production, 1960–1980*

transport distances have increased markedly over the past 20 years, as the forest resource base has visibly receded to the southeast (see Figure 5.2 above).

The key element in the charcoal production operation, the factor that made charcoal the major drain on Sudan's dwindling forest resource, appeared, from this study, to be the process of carbonization. The NEA noted that some 18 cubic metres of growing stock was lost for every tonne of charcoal produced. This was based on the ratios of 3 cubic metres of growing stock per tonne of firewood, and 6 tonnes of firewood carbonized per tonne of charcoal produced.[4] In energy terms, production under these conditions entailed losses of approximately 72 per cent of the initial energy content of the firewood input.[5] Even before the charcoal left the production site, the vast majority of the forest resource input had been lost.

When the ERC drew up its plans for the development of its five technologies to be pursued under SREP, it was assumed that new charcoal kiln design and dissemination would be a major activity.[6] However, since technology development was to be based upon grant disbursement, the ERC first had to learn more about participants in the present production and distribution system, in order to determine who best could utilize grant support, and what sorts of activities could be undertaken by the prospective grantees. Accordingly, the ERC commissioned research into the production and marketing of charcoal in central Sudan.

The ERC was greatly assisted in its research by Sudanese foresters. Dr Hassan Osman Abd El Nour, who had just completed a posting as Conservator of Forests for the Blue Nile Province, a major charcoal production area, was engaged as a consultant to briefly survey production in that area, and to assist Dr Derek Earl, an overseas consultant, in developing a longer, more quantitative research programme for the production sector. Gaafar El Faki, a forest economist and head of the ERC's Dissemination Unit, used his field experience in the Central and Eastern Regions to design and implement a charcoal marketing study, assisted by locally based foresters.

### Initial Field Investigations: Rapid System Appraisal

Drs El Nour and Earl undertook a rapid reconnaissance of the charcoal production sector during January and February 1984. Their work entailed both a tour of major production sites in the Blue Nile and Kassala provinces, and discussions with senior Forestry Administration officials in Khartoum and various regional headquarters.

El Nour and Earl soon unearthed information that prompted the ERC to examine the production system far more closely. First, a review of the forestry literature on Sudan (cited in the NEA's determination of a conversion efficiency of 18 cubic metres of standing forest cut per tonne of charcoal produced) showed that none of these studies contained any empirical measurements of the actual conversion process.[7] No one had quantitatively analyzed kiln operation.

While Jackson (1960), Saini (1964), and Foggie (1967) made small samples of fuelwood consumption patterns in the Blue Nile province, none actually monitored charcoal making itself. Jackson developed an estimate of fuelwood cut: charcoal produced of 17:1 by comparing his forest depletion estimates with Forest Department records of rail movements of charcoal from the production areas. This, of course, was a crude approximation, and Jackson noted that this conversion measure contained considerable potential error.[8] Saini and Foggie quoted Jackson's conversion estimates without further testing, as did a later study by Bayoumi (1983).[9]

The NEA study's conversion ratio of 18 cubic metres of growing stock cut per tonne of charcoal produced entailed a revision of Jackson's stacking factors (growing stock: tonne stacked firewood) and conversion ratios from 2.7–2.9 to 3.0–3.1 cubic metres growing stock: tonne stacked firewood, and 5.5 to 6.0 tonnes firewood: tonne charcoal, respectively.[19] Essentially, these were *ad hoc* adjustments to the old figures deemed necessary because of the obvious changes in the forest resource base from Jackson's time. Aside from the collection of anecdotal evidence from experienced foresters by NEA staff, no new measurements had been undertaken.

The 18:1 conversion ratio, which depicted charcoal making as the major drain on the forest resource in central Sudan, was thus based upon a series of rough approximations and not upon any empirical analysis of the existing production system and its participants. It implied that the present system was primitive and in need of immediate overhaul; but it offered little information about the system itself. El Nour and Earl provided this missing information. Their report from their rapid appraisal tour of production areas in the Blue Nile and Kassala provinces called the assumptions and implications of earlier studies into question.

The history and sophisticated organization of charcoal production operations visited by these SREP consultants led them to question whether processes that have endured over such a time could indeed be 'inefficient'. They noted that the industry contained many long-serving entrepreneurs, with some 25 from the Blue Nile Province possessing over 20 years of experience in charcoal-making.[11] The entrepreneurs employed 50–150 charcoal workers each on a seasonal but regular basis, with most labourers having practised charcoal production for over three years. Some 80 per cent of the workers travelled great distances from their tribal homes in Western Sudan to take part in charcoal making as their dry-season income generating activity. As their income was determined by kiln output, they devoted great care to the carbonization process.[12]

The consultants observed that commercial charcoal making in the area took place on fixed sites agreed upon by the entrepreneurs, landowners, and the Forestry Administration well in advance of the commencement of production.[13] All wood was carefully cut, stacked, and dried before carbonization, and kilns were loaded and covered with great organization and care. The Sudanese earth kilns were far larger than those from other nations, averaging over 100 cubic metres in volume.[14] All these factors set the Sudanese production system apart from the stereotype of earth kiln charcoal production as a small, haphazard, and inefficient operation.

Their rapid review of the industry convinced El Nour and Earl that its history and organization mitigated against the sort of production inefficiencies attributed to it in previous, largely qualitative assessments. They recommended that further quantitative investigation of the conversion process be given priority by the ERC under SREP. They cautioned against the immediate implementation of kiln design alterations or the introduction of new conversion technologies: 'It must be stressed that the charcoal industry at present is providing a good fuel at reasonable price to the consumer with little or no inputs of foreign exchange, and should not be disturbed lightly'.[15]

El Nour and Earl identified two other aspects of the production system that they felt merited further attention. Production sites and charcoal storage depots contained large quantities (Earl estimated up to 20 per cent of charcoal volume) of charcoal dust and fines, which could be converted from waste to viable fuel through some form of densification technology. They also noted that large areas of forested land were burnt to ashes, without any form of fuelwood or charcoal utilization, as part of mechanized agriculture expansion. More resource-efficient land use policies conceivably could reduce such waste.[16]

Their implication, based upon their field observations and conversations with charcoal producers and local forestry and agricultural authorities, was that the charcoal production sector offered more potential innovation pathways than the one of kiln improvement, and that this pathway offered uncertain potential.

## Initial Quantitative Analysis

El Nour and Earl's report demonstrated the limitations of previous investigations into charcoal production, and revealed the importance of achieving a greater empirical understanding of the existing technology. ERC plans to introduce new kiln designs were delayed, pending the results of more empirical study. Some experimental trials on portable metal kilns left by an earlier assistance project were undertaken to train staff in their use and in testing techniques, but the major work centred about a quantitative analysis of commercial charcoal production in the Blue Nile province.

El Nour and a young BSc forester, Kamal Satti, of the Central Forestry Administration, returned to the Blue Nile area to set up the study. From 15 March to 30 June 1984 they observed and recorded production information from five separate production zones, containing a total of 23 work sites and

41 earth kilns. These represented a diverse population of entrepreneurs, labourers, and kiln sizes, as well as a varied forest resource base.[17]

This was the first attempt in Sudan to make detailed measurements in this sector, and as such it was as much a learning process about investigative methods as it was a new contribution to the technical understanding of charcoal production. The main problem encountered was the reconciliation of the data gathering needs of the inquiry with the limited production season. Production occurred only within the December-June (approximate) dry season. El Nour and Satti's sample was large in number and geographically widespread. While such a sample permitted the observation of site and producer-determined variations, it also necessitated methodological short-cuts in order to obtain all the data required in the limited time available.

The researchers decided to base their conversion efficiency calculations on extrapolations of wood input and charcoal output drawn from measurements of sample wood stacks and charcoal sacks produced. Wood input weights and volumes were recorded for stacks formed from various stem diameter groups (0–2 cm, 2–5 cm, 5–10 cm, etc), and estimates of the quantities of wood from each group contained in a given kiln were made. The external dimensions of the finished kiln also were estimated. Sample charcoal sacks were weighed and the proportional composition of lump charcoal, fines, and other materials within were recorded.

The investigation made the first quantitative measures of charcoal production techniques in Sudan, but, because it did not measure total inputs and outputs for any kiln operation, it could not provide a definitive measure of the overall conversion process. When the data was analyzed, it became apparent that any attempt to obtain a figure for wood volume or weight input per tonne of charcoal output would entail adding extrapolations to extrapolations. Volume input calculations depended upon an estimate of kiln size, which could only be crudely approximated from the dimensions recorded by the researchers. They had noted the circumference and height measures, and kiln size was approximated as the volume of a cone of similar dimensions. This geometrical abstraction could differ by as much as 50 per cent from the volume of a spherical section of similar dimensions, another reasonable approximation for the kiln shape.[18]

Wood input weight estimations depended both on the accuracy of the density measures obtained from sample stacks, and on the researchers' approximations of the proportions of wood of each diameter group contained in the kiln. Their accuracy also depended on the assumption that the charcoal producer would stack the billets in the kiln in the same manner as he had prepared the sample stacks. Moreover, no moisture content measurements of wood input were taken, so the energy content of the input could not be determined.

Charcoal output was estimated by taking the average contents of a ten sack sample, and multiplying this by the total recorded sack output. The charcoal producers had no scales, and sample sack weights varied by an average of 4 kg per 39 kg sack.[19] This added an additional potential error of 10 per cent to the conversion factor determination.

The input:output ratio, which reflected a combination of weight and volume estimates, contained a multiplication of potential errors that raised serious doubts as to its reliability. Moreover, the absence of complete measures of wood inputs and charcoal outputs for any single kiln made it impossible to check the validity of any of the assumptions made.

Nonetheless, the range of conversion ratios that emerged from the study, 6–9 cubic metres (stacked) of wood input per tonne of charcoal output, differed greatly from the 17–18:1 figures that had been used in earlier reports on Sudanese charcoal production. The new figures could not replace the old ratios, because of their uncertainty; but they did alert the ERC that the findings of previous work might warrant further reassessment.[20] The ERC decided to further delay any SREP introductory work for new kiln designs until a more comprehensive study could be undertaken.[21]

In addition, the researchers, particularly the young forester Kamal Satti, who would lead the follow-on study, gained useful experience in field analysis of charcoal production. As they noted in their report, 'Lessons learned from this first investigation will allow more accurate and objective measures to be obtained from future studies.'[22] Equally important, they developed a respect for the skills and knowledge of the charcoal makers and the entrepreneurs who co-ordinated their operations:

> Although charcoal is made in earth kilns in Sudan, it is by no means produced by 'primitive' methods. The charcoal production system in the Blue Nile Province . . . is a highly developed network of entrepreneurs, agents and workers.[23]

## Follow-on Study

In November 1984 the ERC and the Central Forestry Administration, supported by SREP and the FAO 'Fuelwood Development for Energy in Sudan' project, began a new charcoal production study to test the tentative results of El Nour and Satti's research. Satti led this study, assisted by an Americal Peace Corps Volunteer, Jon Dorré, and local Forestry Administration staff. The new study took place in the Kassala province, and, like the previous work, used professional charcoal makers and traditional production techniques. The forest resource in the Rawashda Forest of Kassala was similar to that in the Blue Nile province, with the same species, *Acacia seyal,* preferred for charcoaling.

Sati and Dorré's study covered eight kilns over virtually the entire seven month production season (November 1984 – May 1985). Aware of the problems that had faced the previous work, they focused their empirical analysis on the measurement of total inputs to and outputs from this smaller sample. All production took place within a forest reserve, and, prior to the study, the charcoal makers and local Forestry Administration authorities had agreed to allow this new area to be exploited on the conditions that the producers would work under the Administration's direction (the FA replacing the entrepreneur), and that the study's data gathering needs would be respected.

Thus, the new investigation contained an element of user-researcher collaboration not seen in the previous study, which had examined already established production sites. In this study, the charcoal makers gained a new production site close to markets in Gedaref and Kassala towns. The Forestry Administration, through this pilot production exercise, gained assistance in the inventory of the resource content of one of its important local reserves, and in the managed exploitation of this reserve for charcoal production.[24]

The researchers began work at the start of the production process, and thus were able to completely inventory both the forest stands cut for carbonization and the fuelwood that entered the kilns. In addition, they took moisture content samples immediately before kiln stacking, to determine oven dry weight equivalents for the wet fuelwood inputs. This enabled later conversion efficiency determinations to use a more standard, dry weight basis, making comparison with findings in other nations possible.[25] They weighed all charcoal output, so that their conversion ratios were total input:output measurements, and not the combination of sample measures and extrapolations contained in the previous investigation.[26]

**Table 5.1 Rawashda Forest Charcoal Production Measurements**

| Kiln | Area felled (feddans) | Fuelwood standing volume (cubic metres) | Cubic metres/ feddan | Fuelwood oven-dry weight (tonnes) | Cubic metres per tonne | Charcoal produced (tonnes) | Tonnes fuelwood per 1 tonne charcoal |
|------|------|------|------|------|------|------|------|
| A | 14.3 | 111 | 7.76 | 75.5 | 1.47 | 22.7 | 3.33 |
| B | 15.2 | 100 | 6.58 | 67.6 | 1.48 | 20.7 | 3.27 |
| C | 11.4 | 68 | 5.96 | 41.4 | 1.64 | 13.1 | 3.16 |
| D | 8.1 | 57 | 7.04 | 35 | 1.63 | 10 | 3.50 |
| E | 7.6 | 44 | 5.79 | 26.7 | 1.65 | 8.1 | 3.30 |
| F | 6.2 | 38 | 6.13 | 23.3 | 1.63 | 6.3 | 3.70 |
| G | 10.7 | N.A. | N.A. | 56.1 | N.A. | 16.6 | 3.38 |
| H | 9.3 | N.A. | N.A. | 44.2 | N.A. | 13.4 | 3.30 |
| MEANS | 10.35 | 69.67 | 6.54 | 46.225 | 1.58 | 13.86 | 3.37 |

NOTES:  Kilns G and H constructed from small diameter wood (5–10 cm dbh) only
Kilns A through F constructed from more mature forest stands (stems of 5–20 cm dbh)
dbh = breast-height diameter
SOURCE: Satti and Dorré, p 2.

Table 5.1 below summarizes the key findings of the study. The high efficiencies of the Sudanese earth kilns postulated from previous research were empirically confirmed. On average, only 3.4 tonnes (oven-dry) of fuelwood input were required to produce 1 tonne of charcoal, not the 6 tonnes estimated by the NEA and earlier studies. As 4 tonnes of wood input per tonne of charcoal output had been cited in the international literature as the benchmark for an 'efficient' design, this meant that, in thermodynamic terms, the Sudanese earth kiln performance was outstanding.

The study did not record the stacked volume of fuelwood input, as it preferred to use the more accurate weight-to-weight input-output comparison to determine carbonization efficiency. However, given the NEA's own estimate of 3 cubic metres of stacked fuelwood per tonne of fuelwood input, the stacked volume-to-weight conversion figure the study implied is 10.2 cubic metres (stacked) input per tonne of charcoal produced – considerably less than the 17–18 cubic metres input that the NEA had assumed was required. More important, the research threw doubt upon the assumptions made by the NEA and the ERC itself that conversion waste could be dramatically reduced through changes to existing techniques. While the Sudanese earth kiln efficiency was not as high as that obtained in sophisticated pyrolysis and gasification operations, it compared very favourably with the efficiencies obtained from brick and portable metal kilns described in international literature.[27]

The study also found that kilns using smaller diameter wood (G and H in the table) performed comparably to those using the larger stems preferred by the charcoal makers. This production experiment, which had been included in the study at the suggestion of the FAO's forest management expert in Sudan, implied that the 20 year rotations for *Acacia seyal* that had been assumed necessary for reserve resource management could be reduced.[28] This finding urged a reassessment of existing management plans and of the viability of new forest plantations of *Acacia seyal* for charcoal production and other products, which the Central Forestry Administration and the FAO agreed to undertake.

Satti and Dorré concluded,

Considering the high efficiency of the traditional Sudanese kiln, attempts at improving its performance are probably not justifiable. Instead, this report suggests that responsible and organized utilization of the traditional kiln within charcoal production programs can play an essential role in long-term strategies for fuelwood conservation and reforestation in Sudan.[29]

## Charcoal Marketing: Additional Local Knowledge and Skills

While it refined its measurements of conversion efficiencies, the ERC also refined its appreciation of the economic and commercial aspects of the charcoal production industry. Gaafar El Faki Ali, the Dissemination Unit director, studied the charcoal marketing process in central Sudan.[30] His study provided a more detailed picture of the complex system that had been described earlier by Earl and El Nour. He showed that not only was the charcoal production industry a sophisticated commercial activity, involving detailed logistical, labour management, and stock control measures, but it also possessed an elaborate and effective capital/financial arm, derived from the traditional *sheil* lending system of Arabic culture.[31] The seasonal production operation contained what he termed a 'revolving initial capital' mechanism, in which the investor/entrepreneur provided an advance payment to his labourers at the beginning of operations, to be repaid throughout the production cycle as returns from charcoal sales were received. Towards the end of the production cycle the labourer/debtor became a creditor, as his proceeds from production exceeded his advances, and received a share from the income of all further sales. Ali noted,

> The investment can thus be described as self-financing where the initial capital (working capital) is allowed to revolve through reinvestment of returns and mutual borrowing/lending between investor and labour all along the process. Despite all inherent drawbacks, this intricate system has been functioning all throughout the industry's history.[32]

The system had its flaws, particularly in the risks it entailed for the investor at the beginning of the production season, when he undertook large capital outflows to labourers who could, in theory, desert or otherwise disrupt operations. However, it had evolved its own safeguards through the employment of agents and foremen to minimize such disruptions.[33]

This financial system had supported the charcoal production industry from its commercial origins in the 1930s, without the need for any significant bank financing. There seemed to be little likelihood that such 'conventional' financing would be required in the future.[34]

Ali observed that, since the 1960s, charcoal production had become largely a 'salvage operation', in which producers used forest resources that were earmarked for destruction, to make way for agricultural land expansion. Some 84.5 per cent of the charcoal produced in the Blue Nile in 1984 originated in 'commercial production zones', lands defined by government decree as allocated for future agricultural expansion. El Faki pointed out that declaring whole areas 'commercial' and allowing their clearfelling through licensed or unlicensed procedures was antithetical to efficient forest management.[35] Yet, it was difficult to proceed otherwise, without any linkages between charcoal producers and agricultural operations.

Finally, Ali reported that, although this was a traditional industry, as Earl and El Nour had stated, recently it had admitted many newcomers to its production and distribution systems. He found that 46 per cent of the producers surveyed (handling 34 per cent of total production) had worked in this business for less than five years.[36] Some 78 per cent of the charcoal traders surveyed in Khartoum, who controlled 71 per cent of the charcoal distribution from the Blue Nile, were the first from their family in the trade.[37] He speculated that the increasing transport costs due to petroleum price increases and deforestation had put the industry into a period of transition of ownership and control.[38]

In sum, the industry was sophisticated, and not capital constrained. It relied on the continuous expansion of clearfelling and agriculture for its resource base, and the absence of a coherent government management strategy for this resource was a concern. While charcoal production was looked upon as a traditional occupation, it now contained a significant newcomer presence. These individuals might be receptive to new ideas about how the sector could develop. While earlier work had shown that kiln design innovation offered limited potential, El Faki's study showed that innovations to resource management could prove of great interest and benefit to both new and established producers.

## New Technology Development Directions: Resource Management

Satti and Dorré's study did not curtail further charcoal production work. Instead, it set that work off in new directions. While they found that the conversion process offered no simple paths to waste reduction through changes in technique, they identified other areas of forest resource consumption related to the charcoal production industry that offered great promise to conservation efforts and other innovations. Ali's study of charcoal marketing in central Sudan provided further insights into how these new innovation directions could be explored.

The ERC discontinued all plans for work on new kiln designs. The Third Annual Plan for SREP, which covered all work from July 1985 – June 1986, contained no provisions for charcoal kiln design and experimentation.[39] On the other hand, this plan did include two new projects related to charcoal production: the development of briquetting systems, and the incorporation of charcoal production into mechanized farming activities. The CFA's and FAO's work programme contained another new activity arising from the previous investigations: a series of trials of short-rotation *Acacia seyal* cultivation for fuelwood and charcoal production in forest reserves.[40]

### *Mechanized farming and charcoal production*

Reacting to Earl and El Nour's observation that large areas of forest land were burnt to ashes without provision for charcoal manufacture, as a part of agricultural expansion activities, the ERC asked Derek Earl to return to Sudan to collect information on forest resource utilization in the mechanized farming sector in the Blue Nile and Kassala provinces. His study, undertaken in January–February 1985, coupled with the data from El

Faki's charcoal marketing study, provided the elements of a new innovation strategy for this sector.[41]

Earl found that 7.4 million feddans was set aside for cultivation within the mechanized farming sector. Some 3.4 million feddans were 'undemarcated', cultivated without government support and, therefore, without much government supervision. The other 4 million feddans were demarcated into distinct agricultural schemes, licensed and supported by the government's Mechanized Farming Corporation.[42]

Over 2.5 million feddans of these demarcated schemes were in the Blue Nile province, with only 498,000 feddans cleared and under production by 1984. This meant that over 2 million feddans, comprising 13 per cent of the total land area in the province, remained under *Acacia* forest and scrub vegetation. In addition, Earl noted that seven companies held leases for over 2.1 million feddans of the provincial demarcated lands.[43] If there were any possible ways of improving forest resource management and utilization in the province, their implementation would need to consider the interest of these large agricultural enterprises.

Earl talked with representatives of the Mechanized Farming Corporation and several scheme directors, and selected three large schemes, covering 969,000 feddans, for more detailed analysis. In site visits and discussions with scheme staffs he observed that, although their agricultural operations were mechanized, land clearing was done largely by manual labour, with fire used to burn and remove trees and other vegetation. Decisions on which lands to clear and which to retain under forest cover were *ad hoc*, with criteria varying substantially even between sections of the same farm. At best, tree strips were left at approximately 500 metre intervals.[44]

Land clearing operations were carried out by contractors hired by the scheme companies. These operations were expensive, and would cost the companies an estimated LS 220,000 to LS 770,000 over the 1985–1986 agricultural season.[45] At the same time, none of the schemes were using any of the forest resources on the lands to be cleared.

Earl proposed that these schemes and others consider two changes to their current land clearing practices: make charcoal during the land clearing operation, and leave far greater areas of forest standing in the form of shelterbelts, farm perimeters, stock routes, riverbank protection, and shade for worker camps. He argued that both the latter operation would yield a positive economic return in the long run, with charcoal production providing a significant short term gain.[46] The combination of improved land use management and the utilization of resources now burned as waste would greatly increase the overall productivity of the mechanized farming sector, and safeguard the long term future of local soil and human conditions.

El Faki showed that the charcoal industry was sophisticated, capable, and, at present, somewhat flexible, due to its new blood. Earl identified considerable potential for greater energy supply both in the short and long term through reforms to the land utilization practices of the mechanized farming sector. The ERC, through its SREP grants programme, sought to put these two components together, enlisting the skills of charcoal producers and the resources of the mechanized agricultural schemes in developing a long term charcoal production and resource management system.

ERC staff discussed Earl's report with the management of the three schemes studied. Two of the schemes, the Damazine Agricultural and Animal Production Company, and the Arab Sudanese Blue Nile Agricultural Company, submitted grant applications to initiate forest management/charcoal production programmes.[47] Their applications included plans for both charcoal production and selective afforestation measures. The implementation of their programmes would depend upon their collaboration with established charcoal producers in their areas.

The projects began in May 1985 with the construction of small nurseries in the two schemes to provide seedlings for the afforestation efforts. The grants provided for nursery construction and some planting costs, but all charcoal production costs were to be met by the schemes and the charcoal producers, both of whom stood to gain by the new production operations. The scheme managers would decide where and when production operations would take place, and the charcoal producers would determine kiln sizes and carbonization methods. The ERC provided encouragement and assisted in project co-ordination, but the technology users directed the project work, and themselves developed the innovations to be tried in their specific situations.

Without the experience and organizational strengths of both the scheme managements and the charcoal producers it would not have been possible for the ERC to initiate production system innovation on this scale. Moreover, involving these technology users in the project from its commencement increased awareness of its activities in both the mechanized farming and charcoal production sectors. The fact that the participants were investing their own funds in the charcoal production operations increased the likelihood that others would replicate their activities, should production and revenues from initial activities confirm Earl's economic predictions.

## The Redirection of the ERC Charcoal Production Effort: User Inputs Provide a More Productive Focus for Innovation

The mechanized farm charcoal production effort is in an early stage, and the success of this innovation canot be said to be assured. However, it can be said that, as a result of its interactions with charcoal producers and mechanized farm managers, both important forest resource users in central Sudan, the ERC has moved its innovation efforts onto more productive ground. This section discusses how the ERC's findings on charcoal conversion necessitate a re-evaluation of sectoral consumption of forest resources in Sudan, and the allocation of greater importance to consumption due to agricultural expansion than that due to charcoal production.

The NEA's National Energy Assessment drew attention to the charcoal conversion process through its finding that this process constituted over 60 per cent of the total annual consumption of growing forest stock (see discussion in beginning of chapter, and Table 5.2, below). The NEA's analysis of wood consumption, however, contains several errors. When these are corrected, and the charcoal consumption figure revised to reflect the new conversion factors provided by Satti and Dorré, the consumption picture and the relative importance of charcoal production and agricultural expansion change significantly.

### Table 5.2 Forestry/wood consumption and loss: 1980 (NEA and author-modified estimates)

| Consumption/loss | Weight ('000 tonnes) | Growing stock equivalents ('000 cubic metres) | | |
|---|---|---|---|---|
| | (1) | (1) | (2) | (3) |
| Firewood | 8312 | 24937 | 13131 | 13131 |
| Charcoal | 2585 | 46527 | 13885 | 2927 |
| Fire losses | 250 | 750 | 395 | 395 |
| Overgrazing | 290 | 870 | 458 | 458 |
| Mechanized agri-expansion | 363 | 1090 | 4687 | 4687 |
| Shifting cultivation | 220 | 660 | 348 | 348 |
| Other causes (poles, etc) | 170 | 510 | 269 | 269 |
| Total growing stock loss and consumption | 75344 | 33171 | 22215 |

(1) From national energy administration, annex 1, Table IV–20
(2) Figures revised so that all quantities in solid cubic metres
(3) Further revision assuming charcoal production at Earl/Mukhtar, not NEA levels

3 cubic metres (solid) = 1 tonne – NEA
1.58 cubic metres (solid) = 1 tonne – Satti and Dorré
1 Feddan = 1.58 cubic metres (solid) – NEA
1 Feddan = 6.5 cubic metres (solid) – Satti and Dorré
6 tonnes firewood:1 tonne charcoal – NEA
3.4 tonnes firewood: 1 tonne charcoal – Satti and Dorré
Annual charcoal production = 2,585,000 tonnes – NEA
Annual charcoal production = 545,000 tonnes – Earl and Mukhtar

The NEA consumption figures require adjustment in two key respects. First, its growing stock volume consumption measures use stacked, not solid volume figures, based on a ratio of 3 cubic metres of volume to one tonne of fuelwood. A comparison of Satti and Dorré's figures for solid volume and weight presented in Table 5.1 yields a ratio of only 1.58:1, which, when substituted for the former value, reduces volume consumption for all sectors.[48]

Second, the NEA utilizes a figure of 4 cubic metres of growing stock per hectare in assessing the wood consumption of various agricultural activities and fires.[49] While this might represent a reasonable approximation for the stocking of rangelands commonly used for shifting cultivation and grazing, it is unlikely that it accurately estimates the wood content of the choice forest lands selected for mechanized agricultural expansion. A comparison of Satti and Dorré's figures for area felled and weight of fuelwood obtained from Rawashda Forest (from Table 5.1) yields on average of 6.5 cubic metres per feddan, or 3.9 times the NEA estimate. When the higher stocking figure is used in the consumption estimate for mechanized agriculture, its value increases substantially.

Column 3 of Table 5.2 presents the recalculated figures based on the new charcoal conversion ratio and the adjustments to the NEA's volume and

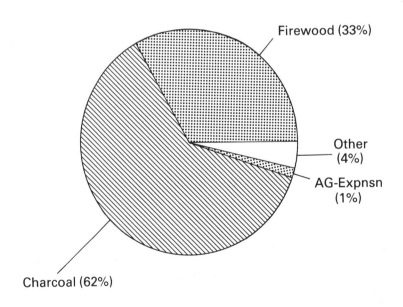

Figure 5.3 *Forest/wood consumption and loss: 1980 (original NEA figures)*

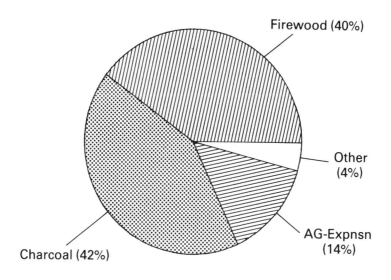

Figure 5.4 *Forest/wood consumption and loss: 1980 (solid cubic metre basis)*

stocking estimates. The charcoal sector's share of total consumption declines from 61 to 42 per cent, while mechanized agriculture expansion increases its share from 1 to 14 per cent. The changing shares are illustrated in Figures 5.3 and 5.4 above.

Further adjustments to the NEA's calculations cause an even more profound change in the consumption picture. The NEA based its figure of 2,585,000 tonnes annual charcoal use for Sudan on extrapolations from household, commercial, and industrial energy consumption surveys carried out in selected areas of Sudan by its staff. This figure far exceeds those derived from Government charcoal production statistics. Earl and Mohamed El Amin Mukhtar of the Ministry of Energy, in separate calculations based upon Central Forestry Administration records of charcoal production, estimated annual production at between 444,000 and 545,000 tonnes.[50] If total forest resource consumption is recalculated using a charcoal sector figure of only 545,000 tonnes, the charcoal industry accounts for 2,927,000 cubic metres of growing stock, while agricultural expansion accounts for 4,687,000 cubic metres, a 60 per cent greater consumption level (see the right hand column of Table 5.2 and Figure 5.5 above).

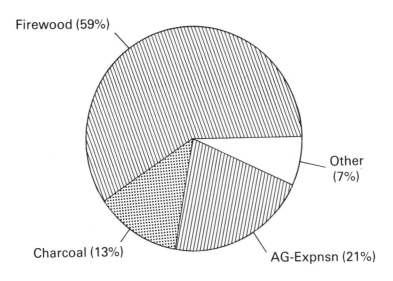

Firewood (59%)

Other (7%)

Charcoal (13%)

AG-Expnsn (21%)

Figure 5.5 *Forest/wood consumption and loss: 1980 (solid cubic metre basis – consumption based on Earl/Mukhtar)*

This result implies that, in the Blue Nile and Kassala provinces, the major charcoal production and mechanized farming expansion areas of Sudan, agriculture, and not the charcoal industry, is a greater threat to the rapidly diminishing forest resource. Moreover, the agricultural sector is responsible for substantial resource waste, as much of the land cleared for agricultural expansion is not utilized for energy purposes at all, but is burned to ashes where it stands, as the NEA itself noted.[51] The deforestation occurring in the area thus represents less of an energy problem than an overall land use management issue.

Thus, the ERC, by moving its charcoal production efforts away from a focus on kiln design towards a concentration on forest resource utilization and management on mechanized agricultural schemes, has applied its technology development efforts towards a more significant area of resource waste. Its new work entails a significant user contribution to this innovation effort, as it represents the product of user interest in both the charcoal production and mechanized farming sectors. For this reason, the likelihood that its grant projects will succeed in implementing new management strategies and minimizing forest resource waste is far greater than that of new kiln designs accomplishing these same objectives.

Work on improved charcoal production in Sudan began with the assumption that new kiln designs would form the centre of any effort to reduce forest resource depletion in the major commercial production areas. However, the ERC's grant-focused approach required that it learn more about technology users in these areas, in order to identify potential grantees and the roles they could undertake in the overall innovation process. In studying the existing production system, the ERC learned that the conversion process was not 'inefficient' at all, and that bringing in new kiln designs would be of limited benefit to forest resource management. Rather than being a liability, the existing system and its skilled producers constituted an asset that could be utilized in reducing the greater sources of resource depletion which, the ERC found, lay not in wood-charcoal conversion, but in land clearing for mechanized agricultural projects.

The ERC's experience in the charcoal production area demonstrates the significant resources of knowledge and skills found in technology users, who all too often can be dismissed as 'primitive' or 'inefficient' due to an inadequate investigation of existing practices. Its work in another technology area, the development of improved charcoal stoves, provides greater insight into the importance of user contributions at all stages of the innovation process, from the incorporation of initial creative ideas into prototypes, to the large-scale public promotion of new model production and use.

## CHAPTER SIX

# Charcoal Stoves: in Sudan The Multiple Contributions of Users – Artisans, Retailers, and Consumers

The examination of the development of improved charcoal stoves under the Sudan Renewable Energy Project reveals specific user contributions to the innovation process, and the importance of these contributions to the success of the overall technology development programme. It demonstrates the ways in which all types of technology users, including artisan producers, retailers, and housewife consumers, can support the design and development of new products. It also shows the importance of pursuing an interactive technology development strategy in order to utilize effectively these important user resources.

The Energy Research Council's adoption of a user-interactive innovation strategy transformed inventive, but not economically productive activity in the stoves area into a successful new technology introduction programme. Moreover, by persuading other local organizations active in stove programmes to adopt a similar approach, the ERC helped make their activities more successful, and achieved a wider dissemination of new stove designs.

## Before SREP: Charcoal Stove work in Khartoum

Khartoum was not the sole site of work on improved cooking technologies in Sudan before the ERC began work in this area in May 1983. Some mission groups and voluntary agencies had initiated stove projects in several parts of the country during the late 1970s and early 1980s, but there was no ongoing production or sales of new designs when SREP began.[1] None of the earlier programmes, although they had achieved a limited production of new stove designs, had succeeded in establishing a self-sustaining production and distribution operation. Several new stove development efforts began concurrently with SREP, under the sponsorship of local and international private voluntary organizations. These programmes will be discussed later in this chapter.

Work on improving charcoal stove designs in Khartoum originated in a workshop on the problem of desertification organized by the Sudanese Society for the Advancement of Sciences in 1979.[2] From 1979 to 1983 a stove improvement programme took shape that, while it did not achieve extensive production or adoption of new designs, developed some important user resources, and established the base of activity upon which the ERC built its subsequent technology development programme.

*Strengths: idigenous knowledge and initiative*
Perhaps the greatest strength of the stove project that SREP came upon
was that it had been a local initiative. Two Sudanese academics, Dr Yahia
Hassan Hamid, an engineer and faculty member of the University of
Khartoum, and Professor Yousif Badri, chairman of the Sudanese Society
for the Advancement of Sciences, developed the initial project around the
former's suggestions for stove improvement offered at the 1979 desertification workshop. Although the World Health Organization later offered
the University some financial support in 1981 to continue its work on
improved stoves, its beginnings were planned and financed by the Sudanese
themselves.[3]

*Early involvement of women in the project*
Another strength of the 1979–1983 stoves work derived from Professor
Badri's other occupation, the deanship of the Ahfad University College for
Women. Ahfad, a diploma institution, was founded by Sudanese interested in furthering women's education, particularly in relation to family
health matters.[4] Professor Badri and Dr Hamid decided that Ahfad women
should take a major part of the testing of the stove models that Dr Hamid
would develop. While stove construction would be handled by the workshop of the University of Khartoum's Faculty of Engineering, all other
aspects of the project would be carried out by Ahfad students, supervised
by Dr Hamid.

This decision helped the project in several ways. The Ahfad women
were far more familiar with cooking practices and needs than many male
researchers. Moreover, in the devout Islamic society of Khartoum, men
were not permitted to enter the kitchen areas of most homes and interview
women to whom they were not related. Any field trials, therefore, required
women to play a major role in data gathering.

Finally, the early involvement of the Ahfad women in the stoves project
provided available expertise and personnel for the ERC when it included
stoves work under SREP. Two Ahfad graduates that had worked on
dissertation projects involving the improved stove designs, Shadia Nasr El
Din and Fadia Mahjoub, were offered work with the council, and the
initial project team was supplemented with a recently graduated engineer,
El Tayeb El Beshir, who had helped with engineering drawings of the most
recent Dr Hamid stove design.

*Weaknesses: insufficient user involvement*
While the 1979–1983 stoves programme possessed the above-mentioned
strengths, it also contained some fundamental weaknesses that prevented it
from achieving any widespread production and use of the stove designs it
developed. Less than 100 stoves had been produced by the time the ERC
became involved in the programme, and all manufacture was done within
the university or by contractors as part of a specific order from the Univer-

sity. Project efforts focused on minor adjustments to past designs, and laboratory testing of thermodynamic efficiency, not on production and distribution concerns. The overall stoves effort, while it possessed invention, in the form of new design ideas, had not achieved innovation, in the form of the widespread production and use of new stove designs.

As will be shown below, the project's chief weakness was its insularity: it did not involve many of the potential users of the technology in its design and development. Women, asked to test new designs, were not called upon to evaluate them, or to suggest modifications. While local artisans produced hundreds of thousands of traditional stoves each year for Khartoum households, they were not consulted about alternative designs or potential modifications. Nor were other metalworkers, whether they operated small welding shops or large fabrication plants, brought into the design development process. It was hoped that these people would eventually be using the new designs in mass production, but it was felt that they could not possibly contribute to their formulation. In fact, there was a belief that the production sector could only 'un-do' good designs.

*Limited women's input*

Although women were given a greater chance than artisans to participate in the stoves project, they were not given a first-rank role in technology development. Cooks, primarily women, provided some initial ideas during design formulation, but were not consulted regarding later modifications. The initial stove research in 1979-1980 found that women liked the traditional charcoal stove design better than three-stone fires or mud stoves, and that cooking speed was an important factor in stove performance. As a result, Dr Hamid decided that design improvements should be attempted within the general physical shape and materials of the traditional, all-metal stove.[5] When new stoves were taken to houses for trial, however, the women were questioned only on whether the design was easy to cook with (a yes or no question) and on whether they believed it saved charcoal. They were not asked for any qualitative observations on the design, or for suggestions on how it could be improved.[6] While the cooks were asked if they would buy their trial stoves, their answers were of limited value. There was no quantity of stoves actually available for purchase, with the prototypes in the households destined to move elsewhere for new experiments. Moreover, the designers and researchers had no idea what such stoves would cost, and couldn't give the cooks a firm price in reply to their queries. The hypothetical question 'would you buy this stove?' was over whelmingly answered in the affirmative, as the response carried no future obligations.[7]

Even the Ahfad women researchers were to a large degree excluded from the stove design development process. They collected information on field trials and laboratory efficiency tests, which they tabulated and reported to Dr Hamid, but they were not involved in forming or producing the prototypes. This remained the exclusive responsibility of Dr Hamid, those drawings were faithfully reproduced as stove prototypes by the technicians in the University of Khartoum's workshop. The message thus indirectly transmitted to the women and their own educational institution was that the University of Khartoum, with its staff of professional engineers, was the sole body that could contribute to design decisions. Even the male professional educators who administered Ahfad could not play a role in this area.[8]

The Ahfad women developed the attitude that their role was to take the design as issued from this workshop, and not to question its physical form. While they had been strong supporters of design changes coming from the University, they wished to discourage innovations from other sources, because this type of change challenged their ideas of how technologies are developed and disseminated. Nor did they themselves suggest or attempt stove construction or design, perhaps because they feared that, without formal engineering qualifications, they could not contribute to stove design improvement.[9]

*Lack of project objectives and management*

The 1979–1983 stoves work consisted of tinkering without much innovation. The design was altered repeatedly, perhaps being improved in the process, but stoves were not being produced or cooked upon in any quantity. The stoves project never acquired a coherent structure or implementation plan. There were no estimated outputs, no timetables, and no budgets. Work ebbed and flowed in response to what money the Government of Sudan and donors like WHO chose to provide.

Basically, this initial work revealed ample intellectual resources, but poor innovation management. The stove project founders had begun to explore user needs, but had then retreated to their laboratory, without examining other users involved with stoves. In particular, they did not examine the needs and capabilities of stove producers and distributors, who would have to play an important role in the eventual widespread development of any design. The programme, by 1983, was moving toward less user involvement, and more attention to solitary laboratory experimentation.

## Initial SREP involvement: May–November 1983

When the ERC assumed responsibility for the stoves project in May 1983 it decided to employ the two Ahfad women and the male University of Khartoum engineer. This provided for the retention of much of the learning from the earlier stages of technology development.

The ERC was eager, because of SREP's mandate to 'commercialize' technologies, to increase the scale of project activities, but it found that a direct move into field production and distribution of the improved design was not possible. The shortcomings of the previous field trials made the

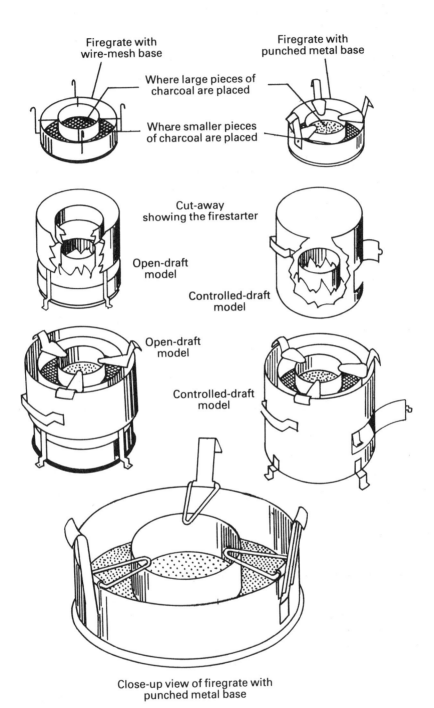

Figure 6.1 *Improved charcoal stove design*

viability of the basic design for consumers uncertain (particularly because of the absence of a real option to buy for the test families). Moreover, Dr. Hamid had revised his design since the last laboratory and field trials, and wanted all further work to utilize the new, as yet untested model. The new model required new laboratory and field testing.

*Laboratory testing*

The procedures of the laboratory testing (primarily boiling water tests) remained unchanged from previous studies. The test did not conform to the recently published international methods, but, in view of the desire to achieve rapid, useful results, consistency, more than method, was deemed important.[10] The Ahfad women quickly organized the materials and equipment and began the testing programme, under their old procedures, whereas initiating a new test method could have caused delays. The new stoves and traditional designs underwent boiling water tests. The researchers looked for a significant improvement in performance in comparison with that of traditional stoves, not an absolute measure of thermodynamic efficiency.[11]

The new stoves tested at 24.5 per cent thermodynamic efficiency, compared to 17.8 per cent for traditional stoves.[12] This meant little in absolute physical terms, because the test results were not readily comparable with those from other nations. However, the 37.6 per cent improvement on traditional stove performance was significant.

The tests showed another aspect of stove performance that improved charcoal consumption efficiency. The new model contained a two-section grille design (see illustration, Figure 6.1, above), that permitted small charcoal pieces ordinarily discarded as waste to be utilized in cooking. The small pieces, placed in the outer compartment, reduced radiation losses from the large pieces in the inner compartment, where combustion would start, only igniting once the overall firebed temperature reached a higher level. The stove required only a small amount of large charcoal pieces to operate effectively, while still providing the quick starting and boiling performance desired by Khartoum housewives.

The stove's operation using small charcoal pieces was an important design feature, as charcoal available in the Khartoum area, obtained from production sites 300–600 kilometres away, contained large quantities of small pieces in an average sack. Rising tranport costs also contributed to the doubling of sack prices between 1980 and 1983. These factors made the new design's use of small charcoal pieces especially attractive for this part of Sudan.

However, boiling water tests could not determine the significance of this innovation. Field trials, in which home consumption was measured, were needed to determine to what extent this design feature improved the utilization of a family's charcoal resources.

*Field testing*

Previous field tests had asked cooks whether they thought that charcoal was saved with new stoves, but they had not involved these stove users in actual fuel measurement. Measuring household fuel consumption contained numerous methodological and logistical problems.[13] The ERC's field test programme sought to obtain data that although approximate, given these constraints, would be useful and available within six months for analysis. To meet these requirements, the users had to help in data collection.

The programme began with a general survey of 300 households in six low and middle income areas of Khartoum. Its purpose was to understand better the basic patterns of charcoal purchase and use, and to identify a smaller sample of families mostly dependent on charcoal for their cooking needs. This smaller group of 96 families (16 from each area) was then offered an incentive to assist the ERC's work by monitoring their fuel consumption over two periods of roughly three months each, the first using their existing stoves, and the second using new stoves. No actual weighing was required. The families kept a record of each sack and *malwa* (mound) of charcoal purchased by ticking a sheet of paper provided by Ahfad women students serving as field researchers. Even illiterate cooks were able to maintain this recording system.

Given the superior thermodynamic performance of the stoves in laboratory tests, and their ability to use small charcoal normally discarded as waste, the field trial was expected to show a significant reduction in charcoal consumption after the new stoves were introduced. Although the presence of festivals, guests, travel away from home, and other factors could influence energy consumption, it was hoped that the three month period was long enough to compensate for such short-term influences.

The initial monitoring of fuel consumption with traditional stoves proceeded well, but the ERC had great problems obtaining 96 new design stoves to replace these after three months' time. Dr Hamid did not wish the design to be shown to commercial producers until it could be tested, so the ERC asked the University of Khartoum Engineering Workshop, the Piaster Vocational Institute, the Military Economic Corporation workshop, and one small metal working shop run by a personal friend of Dr Hamid to produce the test stoves. By the end of six months, at which point all testing was to have been completed, only some 50 stoves had been delivered to the test households. By the actual completion of testing, only 82 had been completed by these four suppliers, all of whom possessed ample tools and labour to execute the entire fabrication task in a far shorter time. In addition, the field researchers complained that some stoves produced were of uneven or inferior quality.[14]

The data from the 82 households contained variations in numbers of days recorded for use of each stove (not the even three months plus three months envisaged in the field test plan), variations in individual stove quality and even materials, and, it was supposed, additional variation due to the different competencies of the six Afhad field researchers.[15] If the ERC wished to produce an international journal publication on the test programme, the only course of action would have been to start again from scratch. But the field trial was seen not as an academic exercise, but as a test of the practical replicability of the laboratory findings, and as an opportunity to qualitiatively assess the reaction of the cooks to the new stoves. The data was collected and analyzed with this utilitarian aim in mind.[16]

The researchers collected information on unit weights and prices for charcoal sacks and mounds in the sample areas. This data, correlated with the consumption information provided by the cooks, yielded the results displayed in Table 6.1 below. The limited accuracy of the measurements was indicated by the fact that mound-only users, who presumably would not have a problem of small charcoal waste, saved more than sack or sack and mound users. Nonetheless, the average savings of 0.8 kilograms, or 24 piasters of charcoal per day was judged by the ERC to be significant. This represented a potential saving of LS 7.20 per month, approximately the price of one sack of charcoal. This LS 7.20 was also twice the average price of a traditional stove. [17] The trial results led the ERC to decide that, in the immediate future, priority would be given to attempting more widespread production and use of this model, rather than concentrating on further design modifications.

**Table 6.1 Charcoal and monetary savings of improved stoves**

| Type of user | Families | Charcoal consumption (kg/day) | | savings | |
| | | traditional | improved | | |
| | (no.) | stove | stove | (kg/day) | (LS/day) |
| --- | --- | --- | --- | --- | --- |
| Sack users | 36 | 3.08 | 2.37 | 0.71 | 0.17 |
| Malwa (mound) users | 5 | 3.1 | 2.08 | 1.02 | 0.41 |
| Sack and malwa users | 31 | 2.81 | 1.99 | 0.82 | 0.28 |
| Average of all users | | 2.97 | 2.19 | 0.78 | 0.24 |

Source: Ali and Huff, Table 2

*Production lessons from field test problems*
The production problems offered several additional lessons for the ERC stove project staff. The vocational school and military workshop had wished to help the ERC, but they had little long-term interest in making stoves, and had only produced them when they had spare time and capacity.

The delays in production and the quality problems encountered with some stoves also showed that, although the basic architecture of the new stove held promise, its material composition and present production structure might not be optimal. While it was based on the traditional stove design, the new model required several different types of metal (sheet, bar, and mesh), compared to the traditional stove, which used only sheet metal (low-grade, scrap sheet). The fabrication of the new stove required both spot and oxy-acetylene welding, in addition to the hand cutting and folding tools needed for traditional stoves.

The relatively small production order for the field test revealed the problems that these changes caused. While the test did not yield solutions to these problems, it stimulated the ERC staff to look for alternative materials and assembly possibilities.

## Greater User Involvement in Technology Development

On 7 November 1983 the Technical Committee of the ERC, the GIT advisors to SREP, and USAID Khartoum staff met to discuss SREP progress in general. The stoves project occupied a good deal of this discussion. ERC/SREP staff mentioned the problems of larger scale production encountered to date, and speculated on possible options to resolve them. One of these was to build new workshops. specially equipped and staffed to produce the new stoves. This method had been used in many stove programmes throughout the world. However, several aspects of this course made it ill-suited to SREP. The biggest obstacle was the absence of capital in SREP's budget to underwrite a production venture of sufficient size and output to make a significant contribution to stove supplies in the Khartoum area. Starting new workshops was an expensive and complex operation, one that may have been suited to a conventional energy development project, but not easily accomodated by a project that was to implement energy activities through disbursements from a small grants fund (the REDG programme).

*Attracting artisans through a stove production contest*
On 1 December SREP's expatriate advisors met again with the USAID Director and Energy Advisor to report on the progress of the technical assistance programme. The Energy Advisor, who had been thinking about the earlier discussion, inquired as to why the REDG programme couldn't be used to offer a prize to the manufacturer who could come up with the best version of the latest stove design.[18] This idea sounded promising, and it was discussed with ERC staff, including Dr Hamid, who approved it.

The decision to proceed with a contest opened up what had heretofore been a fairly insular research endeavour and transformed it into a public technology development and promotion venture. The prospect of working with numerous artisans and metalworkers was exciting, but it also was somewhat disconcerting, as it would require different skills and management procedures from the ERC. Sensing this, the ERC decided to transfer control over the project from the University of Khartoum research staff to its own, newly formed Dissemination Unit (DU), so that further project planning and implementation could serve as a learning process for its young staff.

On 18 January 1984 the DU announced the charcoal stoves contest in Khartoum's two daily papers. Applicants were to submit a finished stove, and an invoice for the supply of 500 more. Three winners would be awarded cash prizes of LS 100, LS 50, and LS 25, with orders for 500, 350, and 150 stoves, respectively. Entries were due on or before 1 March.

*Neighbour country user contributions*
The success of the contest would depend on attracting as many entries as possible. Some 15 inquiries were received at ERC's offices in its first three days, an encouraging sign at the end of January. The ERC called on Maxwell Kinyanjui, from the Kenya Renewable Energy Development Project, to assist in promoting the contest. Kinyanjui directed a user-interactive stoves programme in Kenya, where artisans and potters produced thousands of metal-ceramic stoves in independent, commercial operations.[19] Also, he had started his own stove production enterprise. He was an entrepreneur, and attracting attention and enthusiasm was his principle concern. For the artisans and the ERC staff, it also was significant that he was not an American or European, but a fellow African national, from a country bordering their own.

Kinyanjui travelled extensively around Khartoum with El Tayeb El Beshir of the Dissemination Unit. Together, they visited large sheet metal industrial companies, welding shops, market handymen, and even traditional stovemakers in squatter locations in markets and automobile junkyards. One day after the first market visit had been conducted, the ERC received an entry from a small workshop craftsman who had been intrigued by the stove. His version not only faithfully reproduced the design dimensions, but also increased both structural strength and external finish greatly from the University workshop produced model. El Beshir was absolutely astonished at this display of expertise, and stated, 'Whoever had this idea of a contest, he was very smart.' This craftsman went on to win the contest, and eventually become a trainer of new artisan stove producers, and El Beshir developed such an interest in artisans and their abilities that he spent the bulk of his time both during and after the contest in field observations of stove production, searching for and developing new design ideas and production techniques. Some 28 stove models and invoices were received by the 1 March contest deadline.[20]

Meanwhile, the Dissemination Unit began promoting the awards ceremony to take place on 1 April, after the judging had been completed. Newspaper articles and media announcements increased public awareness of the ERC's work on stove improvement. The D.U. also ensured that senior public officials (such as the Director of the National Council for

Research and the Under-secretary for the Ministry of Energy and Mining) and the media would be present at the awards ceremony, to give it maximum exposure and to show the entrants that the ERC was very concerned with stove improvement by local artisans.

The entries were reviewed by Dr Hamid, Kinyanjui, and the three project staff. With the exception of a few poorly made units, most were of roughly similar energy efficiency. Quality and price varied substantially. In making the final awards decision, a fourth parameter was introduced. Entries had been received from large workshops, small shops, and squatter artisans from various industrial locales around Khartoum. The prizes were given to the best entry from each group, with first prize awarded to a small workshop, second to a large one, and third prize to an artisan working under a wrecked car in the Khartoum industrial area.[21]

The winners were all very pleased with the awards and the attention, and set about making stoves to fill their orders from ERC. The cash awards had not been substantial, but the future profits from the large orders provided a good incentive to produce more stoves. The ERC agreed to pay LS 12 per stove to each producer, per their invoices.

At this stage, the ERC added new efforts in consumer promotion, concentrating on potential stove buyers, to its work on producer encouragement.[22] To build on public awareness and enthusiasm, and to give the winners additional exposure, the Dissemination Unit offered to help them in exhibiting their stoves at a Friday (the Islamic 'weekend' and major shopping day) market near the workshop of the first prize winner. They offered transport for stoves and artisans, and guaranteed to purchase any stoves not sold. The Dissemination Unit arranged for posters and publicity.

The producers and ERC staff arrived at Khartoum's Sajana market on 27 April with 35 stoves. Less than three hours later, all had been sold at LS 15 to LS 20 each, including two that were hot (they had been burning charcoal to demonstrate their utility) and had to be hosed down before being carried away. When prospective buyers asked about prices, ERC staff referred them directly to the producers, who negotiated each sale. General questions about how to use the stove and why it saved charcoal were answered by both producers and ERC staff.

The ERC held a similar demonstration on 17 May at another market in Omdurman, at which 70 stoves were sold. The producers, especially the traditional stovemaker, could see that their new product had market appeal. By 2 June, one month after the first demonstration, this artisan was regularly manufacturing the new design and, in an even more positive development for the ERC programme, at least ten of his neighbours in the junkyard were making improved stoves based on his product.

Moreover, the traditional stovemakers were organizing their own sales and distribution network. When ERC staff sent to collect stoves inquired if any stoves from the order were ready, they received responses such as

'Sorry, maybe we'll have some tomorrow.' When pressed, the artisans admitted that they were sending the stoves directly to the market, where they were receiving a higher price than the ERC had contracted for. They asked if the ERC staff were angry with them for doing this, and they were told that, on the contrary, the ERC wanted them to get the best price they could, and they could sell all they wanted directly in the market.

## Further Technology Development and Promotion

The stove contest stimulated producers to invest their own capital and labour in the production and distribution of the new design. The traditional stove producers, especially, showed an eagerness to work with the invention of Dr Hamid, and by December 1984, some six months after the contest, approximately 500 stoves per month were being made and sold, independent of SREP financial assistance.[23]

At this stage, it was necessary to formulate a plan for further technology development, based on the importance of user contributions discovered during the stove contest. The Dissemination Unit, which had taken responsibility for the stove improvement programme for the ERC, developed several measures during this period to encourage producer involvement and innovation. The Unit's strategy was to establish the ERC, through its SREP funds, as a service organization for these technology users. While not affecting the artisans' autonomy, the ERC would provide both promotional and technical support to their production process. Having established initial linkages with these users through the stoves contest, the ERC would seek to strengthen these linkages in continuing the development and production of the new stove designs.

*Promoting customer awareness and understanding*
Many of these measures aimed at increasing public awareness and understanding of the new stove design, to promote interest and sales. The contest itself had generated substantial publicity, and the Dissemination Unit developed a sustained media campaign to maintain this interest. ERC staff appeared on educational programmes devoted to environmental and science issues, and used samples and slide presentations to clearly identify the new stove. The journalist member of the Unit established good contacts with both the newspapers and television network, and the rest of the staff learned how to develop media programmes, and how to work with cameramen and other technical personnel to make presentations as smooth and entertaining as possible. The Unit staff also gave several interviews and wrote local newspaper and magazine articles on the history and aims of the stove programme.

The Unit decided to give the new stove a name to aid in its recognition and appreciation. It chose *canun el duga*, (stove of the small charcoal pieces), a name which also advertized a key aspect of this design innova-

95

tion. It also produced a short illustrated brochure which introduced *canun el duga* and its use. While the artisans sold stoves at market demonstrations, ERC staff distributed these brochures to purchasers. The artisans received additional brochures to give to their other customers.

*Monitoring*

Unit staff learned which stores were receiving stoves from the artisans, and paid regular visits to their owners to discuss sales levels and to note any consumer and distributor comments. While at first this monitoring process was somewhat *ad hoc*, it was later standardized on a monthly basis with a constant reporting format and content. Most important, staff frequently visited all production sites to discuss production innovations and problems.

The artisans had shown great skill in manufacturing stoves quickly and to a good standard for the contest. Monitoring of their continued production revealed that, as new artisans imitated their neighbours and began making the new design, general product quality declined. Also, in spite of the expanded number of producers, demand far exceeded supply, and shop owners complained that they had to turn customers away, and that they had to accept inferior products from artisans.

The Dissemination Unit noted these developments, and considered its options for managing production and quality control. The temptation existed to strengthen ERC control over the situation through establishing a government workshop, equipped with more sophisticated tools. The producers could be relocated to this workshop, where their work could be more closely supervised by ERC engineers. Alternatively, the ERC could attempt to enforce some sort of licensing or other regulatory procedure which would require all stoves to be inspected before their sale or distribution. The former option seemed expensive, and the latter impractical. Also, both would have restricted the producers' independence, and user involvement in the ongoing innovation process. Other measures were needed, in line with the Unit's user-interactive strategy.

*Promoting user-user interaction*

Programme monitoring had revealed a variation in quality and design standards among producers. Some artisans continued to make stoves of superior quality to the prototypes that had been produced in the University and other institutional workshops. Virtually all artisans had made process innovations to the original design, such as replacing welds with rivets, using lock seams instead of welds for stronger joints, and saving on raw materials costs through using scrap metal resources, which made their stoves cheaper and easier to produce. Yet, the lack of communication between artisans prevented all these innovations appearing in any one product, and design and quality diversity inhibited buyer recognition and appreciation of the new technology.

The ERC again called on Maxwell Kinyanjui, who had encountered similar difficulties in his Kenyan programme. He suggested that a workshop programme be organized to train producers in the optimum production methods.[24] Further, he urged that, as in Kenya, artisans themselves be utilized as trainers in this programme. These craftsmen could communicate on a different level with the trainees than could engineers, no matter how well the latter understood the scientific basis of the new stove design.

The Dissemination Unit staff developed a producer workshop programme for Khartoum. The initial trainees were selected from those presently producing *canun el duga*. The contest first prize winner became the artisan trainer.

Initially this artisan, Jamal Sharbaak, was reluctant to serve in this role. He perceived the workshops as encouragement to his competition. The ERC offered to pay him as a technical consultant on a contract basis to undertake this training role. This indicated to Sharbaak that the R & D organization highly respected both his knowledge and his capabilities, and was prepared to treat him as it would any other technical expert whose services it desired. Presented with the respect and financial incentives contained in the consultant positition, Sharbaak agreed to lead the workshops. Thus, a school leaver became an educator and a key participant in this new ERC educational and training project.

The Dissemination Unit staff managed and supported the workshop programme.[25] Working with Sharbaak, they produced an illustrated manual for stove construction, consisting of pictures, dimensions, and arrows indicating the order of the cutting and assembly process.[26] They produced certificates to be issued to each workshop participant, which provided a token of achievement and also an indication of the ERC's serious treatment of the workshop itself. The Unit arranged for media coverage of the closing ceremony at which the certificates were awarded, which provided publicity and further encouragement for the artisans.[27]

On Maxwell Kinyanjui's suggestion, they also had Sharbaak produce sets of templates for stove component production. These templates eliminated the need to carefully measure each cut and (a commonly observed artisan practice) to guess at adjustments to other components to compensate for an incorrectly cut piece. Sharbaak did not use templates himself, as he took great care in measurement and consistently produced to the proper size and scale. However, the Unit had observed that this was not the case for many other artisans, and they persuaded Sharbaak to modify his training technique to accommodate those less meticulous than he. He received an opportunity to practice teaching the use of templates through a pre-workshop session involving the training of two Peace Corps Volunteers in stove construction.

The initial 15 trainees all came from the junkyard area where the third prize winner lived and worked. By the time of the workshop in November, more than 15 artisans were producing stoves in this area, providing the bulk of Khartoum area *canun el duga* production. The group as a whole selected 15 trainees (space, templates and time limited the number), with the understanding that those not selected would share in the knowledge and materials given to the 15. The only financial assistance offered was an LS 5 daily allowance, intended to compensate for lost time from the trainees' normal occupations. The ERC also allowed the trainees to keep the templates they were given during the workshop.[28] The workshop was held next to the junkyard itself, so no transport difficulties were encountered.

This first producer training workshop, held in November 1984, lasted five days, during which time each trainee was able to complete several stoves. Sharbaak's teaching method consisted mostly of individual example, which seemed well suited to the trainees' needs. Dissemination Unit staff attended every session, and used the opportunity to obtain additional information from the artisans about their production rates and costs, as well as their sales and distribution patterns. The staff also observed how the templates, manuals, and other materials were handled, and later modified these and the teaching programme based on their experience and the trainee's own comments.

Positive results from the training were not instantly visible in the subsequent production from the junkyard. Several trainees abandoned the templates, with some using them to make new stoves. This was simple to observe, as the templates were painted bright blue and pink to discourage this sort of action.[29] Both Sharbaak's and the Dissemination Unit's attempts to get the artisans to work together in a more organized production line met with total failure, with Sharbaak admitting that the artisans, himself included, preferred doing the whole construction process alone.

Nonetheless, the quality of subsequent production from the junkyard area was much improved, and production levels rose. Sharbaak had been able to communicate his ideas about stove design rapidly and fairly effectively to the other artisans. As a fellow artisan, he was sensitive to their needs and their methods, and thus he was able to show and to teach them about the new technology in a way a more academically orientated engineer might not have managed.

The Dissemination Unit staff learned a great deal more about the artisans' methods and preferences from its participation in the workshop, knowledge that would be utilized in subsequent workshops in Khartoum and in other parts of Sudan.[30] The workshop programme thus benefited both stove production and the ERC itself, as the latter developed a greater capacity to interact with technology users and to manage the innovations it sought to promote.

## Geographical Extension of the Stoves Programme

The Dissemination Unit and SREP/ERC staff were well aware that Khartoum represented only a small part of Sudan, and quite early in the improved stoves development programme they considered how they could reach other areas. The ERC was a small organization, with no infrastructure outside Khartoum. Building a regional infrastructure would have been expensive, time consuming, and probably economically unjustified for the sole purpose of stove and other renewable energy technology development work. Moreover, some regionally based organizations already had initiated improved stove programmes, and had manpower and facilities in place to further this work. An additional consideration was that different resource conditions and cooking practices in other areas could present correspondingly different demands for stove design and use.

The question of how to promote stove prgramme expansion was debated in May 1984, when CARE Sudan submitted a grant application to the ERC to support its work on improved charcoal stoves in the El Obeid area of western Sudan (Kordofan region). CARE had been experimenting with improved charcoal stove designs for over one year, and had decided to develop a metal and clay stove based on the design Maxwell Kinyanjui had produced in Kenya.[31] CARE had been working in the El Obeid region since 1981, and had a strong working relationship with the regional Ministry of Natural Resources. It had a Sudanese staff that was very enthusiastic about improved stoves work, and, if its application was successful, it would hire additional local staff to support the programme.

The ERC approved a grant to CARE's stove programe in July 1984. The Dissemination Unit considered how it could best assist the CARE effort, and several key decisions were made. It would not seek to get CARE to work on *canun el duga*. Rather, CARE was encouraged to continue working with the design it had chosen. The relative proximity of charcoal supplies, the preference for mound over sack sales, and the existence of an interested local pottery industry all supported the choice of metal-ceramic stoves for this area. In addition, the ERC staff felt that CARE's technology development work could have useful applications to other areas of Sudan where metal-ceramic stoves could become popular, and where SREP could give new grant assistance.

While it did not push its product on CARE, the Dissemination Unit pushed hard to install its user-integrated technology development process. In September 1984 ERC staff and Maxwell Kinyanjui visited the CARE El Obeid programme. They found that CARE rented a workshop and employed several metal workers on salary to produce stoves. A large quantity of middle-to-poor quality stoves were piled up in the CARE office, and an equally large pile of metal scrap, which could have made hundreds of new stoves, was piled as waste in the CARE workshop. There was good public awareness of the stoves programme in the market area, but there was little entrepreneurial involvement, and sales were slow.[32]

The ERC staff and Kinyanjui explained about the Khartoum programme, and invited CARE to send staff to attend a producer training workshop. They recommended that CARE give up its workshop and production staff as soon as possible, and that it look to traditional stove producers to expand both stove production and sales. CARE already had planned market demonstrations and media activity to improve sales, and it included the search for new producers in its work programme.

It was discovered that, in El Obeid, stove production and sales both occurred in the central market. This was very different from in Khartoum, where the two operations were geographically separate. El Obeid traditional stove producer/distributors, the ERC staff found, were very interested in the CARE programme, but had not been asked to participate in it. The only stove sales in the market were being handled by a tailor, while stove producers and sellers less than a hundred yards away remained outside the development programme.[33] The ERC staff and Kinyanjui suggested these traditional producers be involved in the CARE efforts as soon as possible.

CARE was receptive to these ideas and soon implemented several changes in its stoves programme.[34] Models were brought to the traditional stove producers, and independent stove production began soon afterwards. CARE terminated its lease on its workshop, and encouraged its hired employees to produce stoves on their own at the market.

This new technology dissemination strategy soon bore fruit. One of the producers visited by CARE and ERC began to make both metal ceramic stoves and *canun el duga* (based on a sample shown him by CARE staff), employing several young artisans. He also became a stove distributor, serving El Obeid and other towns and villages as far as several hundred kilometres away.[35] At the end of its one year grant, CARE successfully applied for a follow-on grant to support the extension of its programme to other towns in Kordofan and Darfur regions.[36]

The follow-on programme contained a series of demonstrations, producer workshops, and publications to raise public awareness and comprehension of the use of the new stoves, and a continuation of efforts to enlist traditional producers in new stove construction and distribution. The Dissemination Unit used its publisher and artist contacts in Khartoum to turn CARE's promotional ideas into finished posters, brochures, and other products.

The ERC used a similar tactic in supporting a stove improvement programme in southern Sudan run by the local Community Development Office and Euro-Action ACORD, a European private voluntary organization. ACORD worked with a UNICEF-originated stove design from Kenya, and the ERC, rather than making recommendations on designs, materials, and construction, brought the southern Sudanese staff to Khartoum for one week (through a grant) to observe a producer training workshop and other aspects of its interactive work with stove producers, distributors, and consumers.[37]

Where demand for improved stoves but no stove programmes existed, the Dissemination Unit looked for local government agencies or other organizations that might have an interest in such work. A trip to review forestry activities in the Northern Region uncovered the resources and potential of the Adult Education Centre organization, based in Shendi. This group later applied for and received a grant to organize producer training workshops and to obtain promotional materials.[38] The Central Forests Administration received a grant to promote improved stoves through its extension programe in the Central and Eastern regions. This grant, awarded in May 1985, covered an ambitious effort to initiate stove production and sales through traditional metalworkers and markets in nine towns in these areas.[39] The CFA was assisted by extension support provided through an ongoing FAO project for fuelwood development in Sudan.[40]

Not all grants achieved the sort of rapid initial success seen in Khartoum. The CFA project, in particular, was slow in its inception, perhaps due to the limited capacity and experience of the extension personnel, who were only beginning their FAO-supported extension training when the grant was awarded.[41] Other grantees, such as ACORD, have had their activities greatly constrained by political instability in their area.

Nor has production proceeded somoothly in all cases. The artisans in the Shendi area, which has no major industrial activity, have been hard pressed to find scrap or new metal to make stoves, and large scale production of either *canun el duga* or metal-ceramic stoves may be difficult to sustain.[42]

### Room for Improvement: a Marketing Specialist's Evaluation

In spite of the initial success of the ERC stoves programme, production of new designs does not approach traditional stove production levels in the areas currently under development, and many centres of demand remain undeveloped. Recent sales and producer participation levels are displayed in Figures 6.2 and 6.3, below. Averaging outputs from March to September 1985 leads to an estimated current annual production of 6600 stoves in Khartoum and other centres. The figures also reveal that stove production seems to have reached a plateau after its initial rapid expansion. Producer numbers, which dipped during Ramadan (May-June), now appear to be steadily increasing.[43] As Khartoum alone requires more than 130,000 stoves per year there is ample room for production expansion. (provided that half its households buy one stove annually[44]

The ERC recognized that more production-level work should be done, and it brought in a marketing consultaint to review its improved stoves programme's progress and problems. In September 1985 Arthur Brown of the Georgia Tech Research Institute arrived in Khartoum. Brown, a market research specialist, served in a small business support programme in Georgia. He knew little about stoves, and had never worked in a developing country. However, he knew about users and their importance to product development.

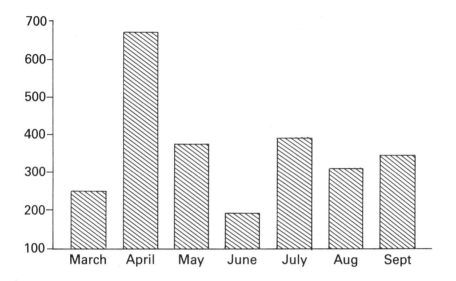

Figure 6.2 *Charcoal stove sales – Khartoum*

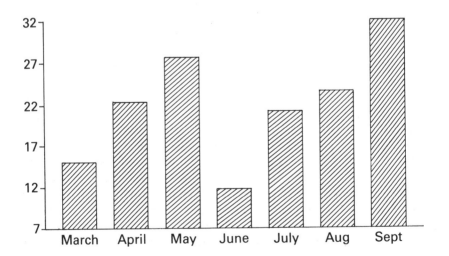

Figure 6.3 *Charcoal stove producers – Khartoum*

Brown examined the Khartoum stove programme, and pointed out that, while the Dissemination Unit had established a close working relationship with stove producers, it had somewhat neglected the other stove technology users, and needed to give them greater priority in its technology development strategy. Market demonstrations, he noted, raised producer enthusiasm, but, because they did not involve local retailers, they contributed to a separation between these two user groups. Producer-retailer co-operation was essential to larger and more widespread sales, so further demonstrations in their present form would be counter-productive.

Brown also noted that, while early field tests had involved cooks and gained essential information from their stove use, these users were not presently being surveyed. The ERC's monitoring efforts were not recording what sorts of people were buying stoves, nor how the stoves were received in buyer households.[45]

Brown recommended that market research be carried out to obtain more information about both the use of new stoves, and the production and distribution systems for traditional stoves. Special attention should be paid to retailers and stove buyers. Also new research should be undertaken concerning traditional stove producers, to better understand where and how they provide the vast numbers of stoves presently sold in Khartoum markets.

## Conclusion

The ERC improved charcoal stoves programme is still in an early stage, but its progress to date has been impressive. It has achieved stove production and sales that appear self-sustaining, as they require no ERC direct financial involvement with the production and distribution process. Without expanding its own staff and facilities, extended its stove improvement programme to applications in six of Sudan's eight regions during a period of just two years. In each new area it brought local technology users into its development efforts, and supported local institutions in encouraging these users to produce and distribute the new stoves. The ERC found that expertise in design, construction, marketing, and even training existed in all the new areas into which it expanded its activities. By delegating responsibility for technology development to local technology users, the ERC could channel their knowledge into the formulation of design and production system modifications that accommodated local resource and cooking conditions. Most important, it could leave product marketing and distribution, which required extensive knowledge of local conditions and preferences, to the expertise of local producer/entrepreneurs, and free its staff to search for new areas for programme expansion.

Although present production is small compared to total stove sales, it is not insignificant in energy terms. If the initial field test results on charcoal savings are correct, 6,600 stoves in circulation will save over LS 869,000 ($289,000, at official exchange rates, as of October 1985, and over $200,000

103

at parallel market rates) worth of charcoal per year for their owners.[46] The stoves, now selling at LS 12–15.00 in markets in Khartoum, although three times the price of traditional stoves, pay back their investment cost through charcoal savings in just over two months.

The stove programme must greatly increase in size and scope to establish the new designs as truly successful innovations in Sudan. The ERC will have to look for even greater involvement of technology users to achieve this aim. The organization has indicated that this is the dissemination strategy it will pursue in this field in the coming years.[47]

Bringing artisans, housewives, and retailers into the technology development process in its stoves programme was, in itself, an insitutional innovation for the ERC. It represented a departure from previous, more insular laboratory-based ventures. This institutional innovation to facilitate a more user-interactive technology development programme was a critical factor in the success of the overall stoves project. As will be seen in the following chapter, such institutional exchange also played an essential role in the ERC's forestry programme, in which new forester-farmer relationships, more so than any new species or forestry techniques, were responsible for the success of new agroforestry projects.

## CHAPTER SEVEN

# Institutional Innovation and Forestry Developement in Sudan

Forestry development, of which fuelwood production is only one component, is less easy to describe in terms of discrete technical or manufacturing issues than is work the areas of charcoal production or charcoal stove improvement. Forestry is primarily a resource development and management-based concern, which can rely on a wide variety of technical options to achieve its ends. The sort of forestry involved in sawn timber production has points in common with village or farm-level small woodlots, but, in general, its attentions are focused on vastly different priorities. Agroforestry measures, such as shelterbelts or forms of intercropping, raise new and still different issues, because of their interaction with food production interests and technologies.

The ERC's support of forestry development in Sudan involved a wide variety of technical concerns in the development of large agricultural scheme, village, individual farm, and government nursery forestry projects. The diversity of its activities was inspired by the wide range of concerns of the multi-disciplinary team of Sudanese experts on the ERC fuelwood/forestry advisory committee, who formulated the guidelines for its forestry programme.

From the standpoint of innovation and the user role within this process, the ERC fuelwood/forestry programme involved little in the way of new forestry techniques or tree species. The propagation, planting, and management methods employed in its forestry projects had all been demonstrated and discussed before, both in Sudan and elsewhere in the world.

However, the most successful parts of the ERC forestry development programme had at their core a change in the institutional structure of the forestry they involved. Their institutional innovations placed forestry institutions and foresters into a more interactive role with respect to the agriculturalists on whose lands the forestry projects were to be advanced. These institutional innovations placed greater control over the nature and direction of forestry projects in the hands of technology users, the agriculturalists themselves, with the foresters taking on a more technical support and service-orientated role. These innovations provided for greater user involvement in the development of the specific forestry technologies employed in the individual grant projects. As a result, the projects received strong user participation and support, and initiated successful tree planting even in adverse environmental conditions.

Chapter 4 discussed the general energy and institutional background to forestry in Sudan. It noted the vast importance of trees as an energy resource; but it also pointed out the loss of central planning and authority over the forestry sector caused by the movement of the Central Forestry Administration (CFA) away from the general agricultural administration activities of the Ministry of Agriculture, and by the confusion and further dissolution of authority and responsibility caused by the decentralization policies advanced by the Sudanese govenment in the 1970s. By the 1980s, the CFA possessed an extensive array of buildings and staff in all regions of Sudan, but it did not possess a communications and control structure necessary to effectively command the resources at its disposal.

Sudanese laws governing land use did not provide much assistance to the CFA's struggles to co-ordinate its activities. Although foresters often referred to central policies mandating the maintenance of a minimum forest cover and resources on all agricultural lands, the multi-layered and often incompatible system of provincial, central, and customary laws provided for considerable ambiguity and confusion as to what practices were mandated in any given area. As Muna Yasin noted, 'different laws apply differently in different parts of Sudan'.[1] It was often uncertain not only what practices were required, but also who was responsible for enforcing correct practices in a given area.

The CFA was further handicapped by the steady erosion of financial support from the central government. The agricultural sector received LS 754 million out of a total authorization of LS 2300 million in Sudan's 1982–1984 Development Plan budget, almost one-third of all development expenditure.[2] Yet, although trees accounted for over 80 per cent of Sudan's energy needs, and represented an essential part of the lives of the vast majority of its people, whose food was cooked on fuelwood or charcoal, forestry was not even mentioned in this most recent Development Plan. Only 0.6, 0.7, and 1.1 per cent of the total budgetary allocation for agriculture during the Sudanese fiscal years from 1982 to 1984 was earmarked for forestry activities.[3]

The ERC recognized that its human and financial resources provided by SREP were insufficient to bring about changes in the overall administrative problems facing forestry as an institution in Sudan. Its strategy, rather, was to utilize its limited means to create examples in which small parts of the existing system could be made far more effective – to establish modest, but replicable projects that could be used to rally popular and government support for more extensive fuelwood and forestry development work.

## ERC Forestry Programme Development

Recognizing that neither forestry work in general nor fuelwood-orientated forestry were new to the Sudan, the ERC began its forestry work by stimulating local foresters, along with agricultural, pastoral, and environmental authorities, to discuss forest energy problems and to suggest ways in which these problems could be attacked. It formed a fuelwood/forestry advisory committee, which met at least once a month from July to December 1983. The committee consisted of foresters, geographers, environmental scientists, range management specialists, and sociologists.[4]

These experts brought vastly different regional interests and priorities to the meetings. This diversity entailed an equal diversity of opinion as to how SREP funds could best be used to increase fuelwood supplies. Some stressed the great potential of irrigated agricultural schemes along the Niles, and their limited utilization to date for forestry purposes. Others felt that work should concentrate on halting the environmental degradation and deforestation plaguing western Sudan, where the southward movement of the desert was destroying fields and grazing lands. Still others thought that projects should focus upon the remaining forest lands in the 'rainfed' (the term used for land which is not irrigated, where rainfall alone was adequate for cereal crop raising) southeastern and southern parts of Sudan, in order to preserve these as sustainable sources of fuelwood supplies.

The experts also differed as to what types of forestry activities should be stressed in addressing the various issues they had noted. Some supported work on large irrigated agricultural projects, while others wanted an emphasis on smallholder farms. Some wanted to support large, centralized government nurseries to rehabilitate and expand their facilities, while others advocated small, community-based nurseries and forestry projects.

This discussion reflected the complexity and regional variation in forestry concerns in Sudan, and impressed upon the ERC the importance of accommodating for this variation in its programme. Its grants system facilitated this accommodation, as it permitted local interests to voice their particular needs and opinions in the application process. The advisory group stressed that the grants programme should seek to support a wide variety of forestry activities, in order to provide for diverse conditions and concerns.

The committee recommended that the ERC's forestry efforts be integrated into local agricultural and pastoral practices. Although Sudan was a large country, with much unexploited arable land, land near sites of food and fuel needs was in short supply, and devoting prime land solely to block plantation forestry was impractical. Increasing domestic food and economic needs required agricultural expansion, even at the expense of forest reserves, and it was unlikely that forestry interests would prevail if they sought to compete directly with agricultural production. However, co-operative activities based upon various agroforestry practices held greater potential for forestry expansion.

Finally, the committee pointed out that substantial resources, both human and material, that could support forestry activities were already in place in many areas of the Sudan. Local technology users, including farmers, herders, teachers, and religious leaders, possessed essential knowledge of environmental conditions and both agricultural and silvicultural practices. Grants could help to enlist this user knowledge and skills into forestry technology development efforts. Their financial incentives could attract farmers and foresters into an interactive, collaborative programme, in which the latter would support, while the former would direct the application of new forestry techniques on their lands.

*The resulting SREP fuelwood/forestry programme*
Acting upon the recommendations of the advisory committee, the ERC sought and approved grant applications under SREP for a wide variety of forestry activities under an equally diverse number of ecological conditions.[5] By October 1985 it was supporting 36 separate forestry projects, with ten additional projects contained in grant proposals under consideration. Of the approved projects, four involved forestry on large agricultural schemes, five involved village and community forestry, 18 supported individual farm forestry, and nine provided for expansion and rehabilitation within Forestry Administration nurseries.

The ERC, through its SREP grants, did not create new categories of forestry practice in Sudan. Agricultural scheme forestry, village forestry, farm forestry, and nursery development all had long histories in Sudan, with some rural agroforestry techniques, such as *Acacia senegal* intercropping, dating back to pre-historic times. Rather than promoting new techniques, the grant funds supported the formation of new institutional arrangements through which established forestry aims and practices could be introduced and strengthened. Most important, the grants to local agriculturalists and community groups served to give technology users greater control over forestry development activities, making them more active partners in project planning and implementation decisions. The grants supported an institutional innovation in which the foresters moved from a policing and dominating role to a more service-orientated function, while farmers and villagers, the local technology users, moved from a position outside of all forestry activities to a central implementation role.

## Initiating Forestry Activities on Irrigated Agricultural Schemes

Forestry activities in the irrigated sector in Sudan dated back to the 1940s, when the first small windbreaks were established to protect fields and canals from dune encroachment in the Gandato, Nuri, and Burgeig schemes in the Northern Region.[6] By the 1980s further windbreaks had been established in several other schemes in this region by its Forestry Administration and the Sudan Council of Churches. In 1951 the Gezira scheme, a 2 million feddan cotton-growing enterprise, began the establishment of small woodlots to provide for local fuelwood and timber needs, and had 7500 feddans planted by 1985.[7] The Rahad Scheme, a 300,000 feddan project in the Eastern Region, included forestry in its original agricultural planning, and initiated forestry activities from its opening in 1974.[8] In fact, the plans of every agricultural scheme initiated since Sudan's independence have included a forestry component.[9]

However, the actual outputs of agricultural scheme forestry to date have been less than impressive, and their paucity revealed problems in the relationship between the forestry and farm sectors. Ali and Sid Ahmed pointed out that, despite all the efforts to date, only 0.3 per cent of the total irrigated lands were under any form of forest cover. Their study showed that the irrigated agricultural sector contained a very limited commitment to forestry or fuelwood development (see Table 7.1 below). Even the Rahad scheme, which began with the inclusion of forestry in its development plans, only assigned the sector enough resources to plant 1000 feddans out of its total of 300,000 feddans developed for agriculture in general.

**Table 7.1 Forestry in the irrigated sector in Sudan**

| Scheme | Total Area (feddans) | Forest Area (feddans) | Portion of Total (%) |
|---|---|---|---|
| Sugar Industries: | | | |
| Halfa Sugar | 43000 | 463 | 1.08 |
| Guneid Sugar | 37300 | 859 | 2.30 |
| Sennar Sugar | 39800 | 230 | .58 |
| Assalya Sugar | 33000 | 340 | 1.03 |
| Kennana Sugar | 32000 | 450 | 1.41 |
| Large Agricultural Schemes: | | | |
| Gezira/Managil | 2100000 | 7500 | .36 |
| Rahad | 300000 | 1000 | .33 |
| Agricultural Corporations: | | | |
| Suki | 120000 | 600 | .50 |
| Halfa | 455000 | 1850 | .41 |
| Abu-naama | 30000 | 300 | 1.00 |
| White Nile | 360000 | 600 | .17 |
| Blue Nile | 300000 | 95 | .03 |
| Northern | 92300 | 940 | 1.02 |
| Khartoum Province: | | | |
| Large schemes | 147218 | 60 | .04 |
| Small farms | 87373 | 22(est) | .03 |
| Totals | 4176991 | 15309 | .37 |

Sources: Ali and Sid Ahmed, p 129; Clarkin, ed, p 132; author calc.

*Opposition to forestry expansion in central Sudan*

An additional problem was the foresters' perception of hostility to further tree planting on the part of scheme agricultural management. Bayoumi observed that the limited afforestation that had occurred in the Gezira scheme originated only after farmers had facilitated an outbreak of black arm cotton disease through the illegal storage of cotton stalks for cooking fuel.[10] Small eucalyptus plantations provided firewood and poles to replace the cotton stalks, and the farmers could burn their stalks promptly after harvesting the cotton, as directed by the scheme. Moreover, because the scheme had not been designed for the inclusion of forestry, the new planting tended to be concentrated on sites unsuitable for crops or adjacent to the ends of irrigation canals, where water supplies were irregular.[11] Forestry was carried out away from prime agricultural areas, and it was undertaken by CFA staff in isolation from the work of the scheme's agriculturalists. The scheme managers, Bayoumi claimed, pointedly resisted new plantings that would achieve a greater interaction between trees and crops, because these, they argued, would open up great dangers from birds and would inhibit aerial crop spraying.[12] Whether or not Bayoumi's interpretation of the scheme's anti-forestry bias was correct, it was a view shared by many Sudanese foresters.[13]

The author's own observations of agricultural scheme forestry reinforced the above impressions of its low state of development, and exposed other problems in the forestry-agriculture institutional relationship. In addition to the limited amount of land devoted to forestry in such areas as the Gezira scheme, the condition of many of the plantings that did exist was deplorable. Irregular water supplies caused tree death or stunted growth. The absence of proper thinning and other stand management measures depressed annual growth and, hence, the value of the existing woodlots for the scheme. It appeared that the Gezira foresters were having difficulties in maintaining their activities at their existing low levels, making significant expansion of forestry under the present management system problematic. Forestry activities in irrigated schemes in the Northern Region evidenced similar difficulties.[14]

The ERC, as it began its forestry development programme, saw that forestry and agricultural institutional interests were heading in opposite and antagonistic directions, to the detriment of the forestry programmes. Forestry operations were becoming increasingly isolated from general agricultural practices. With strong government support for agriculture, but limited support for the isolated forestry sector, the future for irrigated scheme forestry looked bleak. The irrigated agricultural lands held great potential for forestry and fuelwood production, but this could not be realized under present institutional conditions. Changes were needed in order to bring forestry and agricultural interests closer together, and to utilize the knowledge and resources of the latter to devise and support forestry intiatives to benefit both fuel and crop development.

*The Seleit grant project*

Many innovations have originated with accidental occurrences, and the first ERC forestry grant project began in this way. In July 1983, the ERC forestry advisor and the author were searching for an irrigated site that could serve as a base for trials of agroforestry techniques. Having heard that the Sudanese government might be making new lands available on the 11,000 feddan Seleit scheme, located only 10 kilometres north of Khartoum, they met with the scheme manager to discuss the matter. Before their R & D intentions could be fully explained, the manager surprised them by stating how much he thought forestry could contribute to the scheme as a whole, and how he would like their help in getting forestry activities started. He offered to pay for some seedlings from Khartoum nurseries if his staff could be shown how to plant them. On 7 August the ERC forester and the author brought 500 seedlings out to Seleit, where they were planted in two windbreaks adjacent to the project's future poultry area. Although the seedlings were of uneven quality, and represented an *ad hoc* assortment of species because of the paucity of supplies in Khartoum nurseries, most survived, and the scheme manager planed to continue this forestry work. He eventually prepared a grant proposal for the ERC (with guidance from the ERC forester), which was reviewed and approved on 15 November 1983 – the first grant to be issued by the ERC.[15]

Physically, there was little novelty about the forestry work that was initiated on the Seleit scheme. A nursery was built, and a variety of afforestation measures, including shelterbelts, woodlots, shade and amenity plantings were established. A forestry team, consisting of three trained foresters and six labourers, was formed and given an office. Also, a long term forestry plan for the scheme was developed. All of these measures had occurred on other schemes.

However, the central difference in the Seleit project concerned the relationship of the foresters to its agricultural management. The grant was issued to the scheme, not to the local forestry authority, so all expenditures and decision-making powers rested with the agricultural managers. The ERC forester, a retired official from the CFA, arranged that the foresters who worked on the grant project would be placed under the control not of the local forestry body, but of the Seleit director. They reported to him, and received incentives for good work from him, through the SREP grant. This was the first time that Sudanese foresters were engaged in service to any agricultural authority. The fact that the Seleit scheme was a private concern made the arrangements even more innovative. The CFA was wary of the proposal at first, but accepted it as a trial, perhaps because it realized the need to explore new methods for expanding its activities.

The impact of the new working relationship was felt in several aspects of the forestry work on the Seleit scheme. The foresters were able to utilize scheme land preparation equipment to hasten the establishment of new plantings. The agricultural manager, who determined where and when plantings would take place, did his best to ensure that adequate irrigation was made available. Scheme guards provided protection for young trees as part of their general agricultural work. Occasional mishaps occurred, with scheme sheep and cattle browsing forestry sites at times, but most sites remained undisturbed, despite the proximity of large animal populations.

The foresters, too, adapted their work to reflect needs expressed by the scheme's agriculturists. They raised shade and flowering tree seedlings in the scheme nursery, which served both to make the scheme environment more pleasant, and to generate supplemental income for its operations, through seedling sales in Seleit's Khartoum produce outlet. Being around agriculturalists encouraged the foresters to try food and tree intercropping, and they successfully interplanted 20 feddans of eucalyptus with *karkedeh*, a hibiscus species used for drinks in Egypt and Sudan. Sales of the first crop raised over LS 10,000 for the scheme.[16]

*Seleit programme benefits*

The initial two years of work on the Seleit project have been highly successful. Over 100 feddans of woodlot have been established by a staff of only nine men, with the occasional assistance of agricultural machinery operators. This constituted 1 per cent of the total scheme area, in comparison to the 0.3 per cent of the Gezira scheme that had been afforested in the 35 years since 1951 by an entire provincial forestry department.[17] The forestry development plan for Seleit, which, so far, has proceeded according to targets, called for a total of 800 feddans of woodlot to be established, plus other shelterbelt and canal plantings. The woodlots alone would constitute 7 per cent of the total available agricultural area. As this plan was drawn up by the scheme's agricultural management, in consultation with its foresters, its prospects, provided the scheme itself endured, were good.

An accurate cost-benefit analysis of the Seleit project would be difficult to compile, due to the absence of complete financial input data (particularly concerning the scheme's own contributions, which were not accounted for separately in its fiscal system). However, a rough comparison of the inputs and estimated outputs of the work to October 1985 yielded very encouraging findings. The ERC provided the Seleit scheme with LS 66,000 in financial assistance through two one-year grants, which provided for nursery materials and construction, forester incentives, transport assistance, and, in the first year, some supplemental labour support (Seleit agreed to provide six labourers from its own agricultural budget in the second year). The CFA paid the salaries of two scheme foresters, which was approximately LS 6000 per year in total. The scheme furnished mechanical support for land preparation and irrigation, transport maintenance and fuel, labour for planting and guarding, and irrigation water.

Seleit possessed 100 feddans of Eucalyptus woodlot. While the value of this resource in four years' time is uncertain in Sudan's rapidly depleting forest resource situation, 1985 sales by tender of standing forest lots at the Guneid Sugar Corporation, 100 kilometres south of Khartoum, yielded an average price of LS 7000 per feddan.[18] This represented a total value of LS 700,000 for the present standing crop at Seleit, which required only periodic watering and guarding between the present time and its eventual harvest. Continued sales of *karkadeh*, seedlings, and other intercropping products would provide additional income for the scheme during the interim period. *Karkadeh* alone could provide some LS 100,000 per year if the results of the initial 20 feddan trial could be replicated over the existing 100 feddans for two crops per year (the normal cultivation practice for this product).

The Seleit project had other, indirect benefits in the form of practical education and training for both the foresters and the agriculturalists on the scheme. This training was especially important for the foresters, who had limited opportunities to do hands-on work during their university or polytechnic education, due to shortages of funds and transport. When the ERC Director met with the CFA acting Director in September 1985 to inquire as to whether similar arrangements could be made with other agricultural scheme forestry projects, he received the CFA's enthusiastic support for more such work.[18] Equally important, the Seleit Director has been influential in promoting the virtues of irrigated scheme forestry-agriculture integration to his agriculturalist colleagues.[19]

## Village and Community Forestry

The ERC had been encouraged to support community forestry by its advisory committee. It was aware that village-level forestry work was already underway in Sudan. In order to avoid duplication of effort and of error, the ERC reviewed some of the major work in this area before developing its grant programmes. Its review focused on community forestry work in the northern Kordofan Region, and, in particular, on the United Nations-supported 'Restocking the Gum Belt for Desertification Control' project.[20]

*Gum Belt community forestry*
The cultivation of *Acicia senegal*, the trees producing gum arabic sap, was a traditional agroforestry practice in this region. The trees, as well as providing an important trade product for farmers and herders, also improved local agricultural conditions through nitrogen fixation and wind and water erosion control. Trees were grown on approximately a 20 year rotation, with tapping occurring after five years, and with food intercropping customary during the first few years of tree growth. The farmers' 'gum gardens', scattered throughout the area of Sudan between 10 and 14 degrees north latitude, were models of agriculture-forestry integration that

dated back to pre-historic times. However, drought and declining real prices for gum arabic had resulted in declining production and cutting of trees for fuelwood. The United Nations project sought to restore tree cover and revitalize the gum trade.[21]

The ERC foresters toured the northern Kordofan area from 6 to 13 February 1984, visiting UN project operations in the Al Ghabsha, Um Ruwaba, Er Rahad, El Obeid, and Bara areas.[22] They did not examine all UN project installations, but subsequent conversations with CARE foresters, who had greater experience in this region, confirmed the ERC foresters' basic findings.

The most surprising finding of the tour was the low establishment rate of the *Acacia* seedlings. The ERC party did not visit any farm with more than a 20 per cent survival rate. This may have been due in part to adverse rainfall conditions, but the sites showed clear evidence of other, less intractable problems, such as animal browsing, improper or late planting, and complete seedling abandonment. Some gum gardens had seedlings planted with their polythene tube casings still attached, which had prevented growth in the dry conditions. Others had stacks of unplanted seedlings lying dried out in piles in the corners of fields. One farmer who had requested and diligently planted seedlings was quite disturbed when the ERC foresters informed him that he had received *Acacia mellifera*, not *Acacia senegal*, and this species would not produce a marketable gum.[23]

Discussions with local farmers and foresters revealed several organizational and institutional problems. Despite the presence of new Land Rovers and lorries, furnished through UN support, seedlings were not being delivered to farmers at the proper time for planting, immediately after the seasonal rains. Also, the farmers were receiving a number of seedlings calculated by UN programme foresters to plant their entire landholding in a 4-by-4 metre spacing. While this was a correct calculation for their eventual seedling needs, planting an entire farm in one season often was impractical, particularly as other agricultural needs were pressing and the planting season was short.[24]

Overall communication between foresters and farmers in the programme was sporadic and ineffective. The foresters spent the bulk of their time in and around their central nurseries, caring for seedlings, while the farmers spent most of their time in their villages. Brief interaction occurred during village and farm selection, and seedling delivery, but only limited field visits occurred both before and, more importantly, after tree planting had begun.[25]

The central problem was that, in spite of its reputation, this was not a 'community' forestry project. It was largely a tree propagation endeavour carried out within centralized forestry facilities, bringing in farmers only at a very late stage of project development, at which point little could be changed to adapt to local human or environmental conditions. As such, it failed to effectively channel the considerable material resources provided by the United Nations and local user skills and knowledge of forestry into the formulation of a practical and productive programme.

The ERC foresters resolved to seek a more user-interactive forestry development strategy in the formulation of its community forestry projects. User involvement would be fostered by investing the basic responsibility for project design and implementation in the communities themselves, using the grants programme.

### A new approach: the Um Inderaba village project

The ERC foresters initiated this user involvement at the conclusion of their northern Kordofan mission, when they visited the village of Um Inderaba, a site recommended by the advisory committee for community forestry project development.[26]

Um Inderaba village was located at roughly 15 degrees north latitude, north of the gum-growing area, with an annual rainfall of only 150–200 millimetres. The villagers depended on their large *wadi* (depression, with a low-head underground water supply), with its numerous shallow wells, and the area's one working government diesel borehole well for drinking water. The recent drought had virtually emptied the former water source, and the latter was afflicted with periodic mechanical failures and delays in service due to the remoteness of the village from Kordofan government offices.

Um Inderaba lay along the major livestock route between western Sudan and the markets of Khartoum, and herders and their stock often would break their journeys there. The villagers generated much of their income through selling water, food, and retail goods to passing nomads (the food and goods were usually obtained from Khartoum). The drought had severely depressed this trade, and also brought weak and ill herders to the borehole, as other watering sources were exhausted. This congregation of humans and animals further depleted dwindling local fuelwood and fodder resources.

The villagers felt that their environment was decaying, and they were particularly troubled by damage caused to houses and fences by windblown sands from the north. They had discussed the idea of a community forestry project with members of the ERC's fuelwood advisory committee who had visited Um Inderaba in September 1983.

The ERC foresters proposed that the village committee consider what sort of forestry it would undertake if the ERC provided it with an SREP grant of approximately LS 10,000. This offer caused initial confusion, first because it was unusual for foresters to ask villagers what they wished to do, and second because the villagers, familiar with the UN programme, had expected a far more capital-intensive type of project.[27] The ERC foresters, with some difficulty, explained that theirs was to be a different type of project, in which the villagers would take the lead in designing and implementing their own forestry programme.

115

The ERC party stayed in the village for two days, discussing the grant project idea further. The villagers, led by their *sheikh* (religious leader), after some acrimony, eventually decided that some assistance was better than nothing, and began to prepare a proposal to submit to the ERC.[28] The villagers eventually sent two proposals to the ERC for consideration, one for a LS 10,000 project, and another for a LS 25,000 that consisted of the former plan plus additional funds to rehabilitate one of their two village borewells. The ERC Technical Committee, which had been briefed by the touring party, approved the smaller proposal, although it later added the borewell funds in a supplementary grant, after the village demonstrated its commitment to and success in meeting the smaller project's goals.[29] The funds were disbursed to the village *sheikh*, and ERC foresters arranged for periodic consultations and field visits to assess project progress.

## Institutional innovation and Um Inderaba accomplishments

Um Inderaba had almost no physical resources to draw upon. Normal conditions there were harsh, and during the 1982–1985 drought there was no measurable precipitation in the area. At the same time, its population declined, due to death, disease, and out migration, from 2000 to roughly 600 families. The local CFA representative, although 'based' in Um Inderaba, spent little time there, and was of little help to the villagers' project. The ERC foresters could visit this remote site only every two to three months, and greater gaps between visits occasionally occurred.

Despite these formidable obstacles, by the end of its first grant period, the village had accomplished all its objectives, and still had funds in hand to continue its forestry work. It had established a nursery and raised two stocks of seedlings. It had planted and protected a three feddan windbreak with close to 100 per cent survival among *Prosopis* species, and had fenced off 1 feddan in its *wadi* to encourage natural forest regeneration in the absence of animal browsing.[30]

The village had finished its work under its budget estimations because, being responsible for its own materials procurement, it had managed, through shopping around and lobbying the regional government, to obtain substantial concessions on sand, cement, wire, and other basic supplies for its project. The ERC, had it tried to implement the work itself, could not have performed it so economically.

The village had kept its trees alive in spite of the complete lack of rain, and in the presence of large animal herds, by hand watering each tree with donkey cart-transported water, and by establishing a village guard rota to protect the plantings (including a village-devised compensation scheme for the guards). Tree survival spoke well of the drought tolerance of *Prosopis* species, but it spoke even better of the capacities of the villagers themselves.

The village used its nursery to raise good windbreak species, like *Prosopis*, and other species for other purposes, such as neem (*Azidirachta indica*) for shade, and *Acacia* and *Zizyphus* species for fuel and fodder.

116

People built brick shelters to protect shade plantings around their homes from animal damage. The village committee, noting the limited supplies from the nursery, introduced a penalty system for any shade trees that died, adding new incentives to protection efforts.

The existing plantings, by themselves, did not represent a substantial contribution to the welfare of the village or its people. A 3 feddan windbreak, even at maturity, would provide negligible control over sand encroachment for the village as a whole, with a strip of at least ten times its length needed to have a significant impact on local environmental conditions. However, the village had established a means and a method to move incrementally towards these greater technical changes to its environment. The Um Inderaba example also inspired other villages to undertake similar community-organized projects, and the ERC has granted several new village forestry grants based on this initial project.

*Other ERC community forestry projects*

The ERC began several other community forestry projects between June 1984 and September 1985. Ironically, in the two projects believed to have the greatest potential, progress to date has been disappointing, despite the ERC's provision of greater technical support to these efforts than it had furnished to the Um Inderaba project. In retrospect, it appears that this performance disparity can be related to the relative lack of institutional innovation, involving the relationship between forestry and community authorities, in these two projects.

The projects took place in Um Tureibat village in the Gezira scheme, and in El Khwei village in the gum-growing area of western Kordofan Region. Both villages had far greater rainfall than Um Inderaba (approximately 400–800 millimetres per year, versus 100–200 millimetres, on average), and Um Tureibat had the additional resource of Gezira scheme irrigation supplies. With more water, the villages could support a wider variety of tree species, and, in theory, could achieve higher growth rates with no requirement for supplemental hand irrigation, as was necessary in Um Inderaba. Moreover, irrigated agroforestry in Um Tureibat could improve crop yields through providing shelter and reducing evaporative losses, while gum obtained from *Acacia senegal* raised in El Khwei forestry would provide a valuable income, in addition to fuel, for local farmers.[31]

The ERC observed the potential of these two sites, and made special arrangements, upon approving grants to the villages, to provide extra support to their forestry efforts. A US Peace Corps volunteer forester was stationed in Um Tureibat to help with nursery establishment and forestry extension, and a CFA forester stationed in El Khwei was paid an incentive to assist the villagers in building and operating their nursery. The assumption made was that this greater support would accelerate project progress and facilitate its replication in nearby villages.[32]

In practice, neither of these things occurred. The nursery in Um Tureibat was completed, and 20,000 seedlings raised, but the volunteer noted that it was difficult to get the villagers involved in its operation.[33] In addition, he had to obtain an ERC vehicle to carry seedlings to neighbouring villages in order to get the prepared seedlings planted, as few farmers were coming to the nursery (although most had access to adequate transport and finances to obtain seedlings in this far wealthier area than Um Inderaba).

In El Khwei the forester and the schoolmaster, who headed the village project, successfully constructed a nursery and raised some 17,000 *Acacia senegal* seedlings by July 1985. Good rains came for the first time in years, and the surrounding fields were planted with millet and sesame, presenting an ideal situation for *Acacia senegal* planting. However, when the author, a CARE forester, and the ERC forestry advisor visited the area in August 1985, they discovered that no seedlings had been taken to the fields for planting.[34] The planting season was almost over, so promoting seedling sales was not practical. The ERC staff called a farmers' meeting, and offered to deliver seedlings free the next morning to any farmers that came to the nursery to direct the ERC vehicle to their land holdings. Several farmers stated at this meeting that they had not known that seedlings were available before this time. Some 2,000 seedlings were delivered the next day, before the ERC staff had to move on to other villages. It is assumed that little additional planting occurred using the remaining seedlings. Here, as in Um Tureibat, the project had not attracted a true community involvement, and as a result was doing poorly in spite of highly favourable environmental and economic conditions.

Although physical, social, and economic conditions were very different in all three grantee villages examined, making any attempt to compare project progress between them tentative at best, the two villages which received the greatest continual forester presence and attention did less well than the village that had the least forester assistance. While the foresters themselves did their technical assignments well and acted in good faith to advance the project, their constant presence discouraged the communities from taking greater responsibility for and control of their grant projects. Although the more advantaged communities, held the funds required for nursery establishment and planting assistance, they, unlike Um Inderaba, had to acknowledge the presence of a forester paid and supported by another institution. The foresters, by their presence, brought an external authority into the project picture. Intimidated by this official presence, the villagers tended to allow the foresters to implement the projects, and declined to get involved themselves.

In retrospect, it may have seemed, to the villagers, as if the ERC had included the foresters in the two village projects in order to keep the projects in line with its expectations. This perception may have provided a strong disincentive for local participation. The traditional relationship between foresters and villagers in Sudan, as in many other nations, was more that of a policeman and a suspect than that of a benevolent 'change agent' and his clients. The foresters, who were not trained as teachers, but as technicians, saw their assignment as to make sure the grant was carried out according to plan; so, if villagers didn't arrive to carry out necessary operations, they went ahead and did them themselves – unconsciously reinforcing the villagers' impression that they did not have to pitch in and help themselves, for the work was beyond their control. The Um Inderaba villagers, who had no such support, had no such impressions, and organized themselves to accomplish their goals and, equally important, to call on the ERC foresters for advice when their knowledge could be useful to guide further village action.

## Individual Farm Forestry

By October 1985 the ERC, through SREP grants, supported 18 individual farm forestry projects. While these projects represented the largest number of grants in the overall forestry sector, and were estimated to occupy, at that point, some 40 per cent of ERC staff forestry time, their results were not as encouraging as those of work in the agricultural scheme forestry and village forestry areas.[35] In retrospect, their relative lack of success can be seen as a reflection of the lesser amount of institutional innovation they entailed.

The ERC's methods and goals in its individual farm forestry work were straightforward. Much irrigated land in central Sudan was devoted to small (less than 20 feddan) farms, including the individual smallholder plots in the Gezira and other major irrigation schemes. Most of these small farmer holdings could, but did not, support some form of tree planting, ranging from border rows to small woodlots. The ERC felt that, if it could get some farmers to initiate tree planting by providing partial financial assistance through its SREP grants, their example would inspire neighbouring farmers to do the same.[36]

*Soliciting farmer interest through grants*
On 21 September 1983 the ERC placed an advertisement in the Khartoum press, offering to provide financial assistance for tree planting on small private farms. The ERC's grants would help pay for seedlings and, in cases where the farmers were devoting extensive land to planting or constructing nurseries, would provide additional partial capital assistance for tree propagation. The initial response to the advertisement was strong, with nine farmers placing grant applications within the 15 day period specified. Afterwards, the ERC's offices continued to receive a small but steady stream of new farmer applications, which was maintained until the author's departure in October 1985.

While the advertisement succeeded in establishing farmer interest in the ERC grants programme, the resulting grants were less successful in establishing and replicating small farmer forestry activities. At a meeting of 21

August 1984, after the disbursement of ten grants, with 15 applications pending, the ERC foresters reported that only four farms had begun tree planting.[37] Farmers were keen to receive financial assistance, but they were not showing equal enthusiasm for project implementation. Drought conditions were partly to blame, as low river levels had left many farms without sufficient irrigation water for any form of agriculture. However, one year later, after greater rains had remedied this problem, the tree planting situation on these farms had not improved substantially.[38]

During the August meeting, the ERC Director noted that, if the goal of this grants programme was to set an example for other farmers to follow, then, rather than giving out more grants, the ERC should hold new applications until more progress was made on the initial projects. He queried whether further financial assistance in the Khartoum area for such projects would be useful, as the ERC was also supporting local nurseries, and providing free seedlings to farmers through grants could discourage others from going to the nurseries to purchase seedlings.[39] Indeed, the continuing influx of new applications seemed to indicate the farmers' enthusiasm for a free handout of any sort, rather than a desire to support farm forestry, based on their slow implementation of subsequent planting activities. The ERC suspended the consideration of further small farmer grants in the Khartoum area, although it continued to support a small number of new small farm forestry projects in other regions.

*Grants not facilitating user involvement in innovation*

A major problem with the small farmer programme appeared to be that, in this case, the grants device provided the wrong message to farmers. It had been assumed that a small financial input would remove whatever reluctance had retarded farmers' inclusion of trees into their agricultural systems. Instead, the farmers, feeling that they had been awarded a prize, tended to sit back and wait for the ERC foresters to deliver it to them. The ERC foresters noted that farmers were difficult to contact, and did little work on their projects when the foresters were not present.[40] This was in sharp contrast to the attitude of the Um Inderaba people, who would travel for hours over rough roads to come to Khartoum to obtain new funds, or to ask questions about technical problems.

## Government Nursery Assistance

Some 50 per cent of all SREP forestry grant funds disbursed by October 1985, approximately LS 115,000, supported large, centralized nursery development, with over LS 80,000 of this involved in the expansion and rehabilitation of two nurseries in the Khartoum area. The ERC forestry advisory committee had noted, quite logically, that, in order to encourage local farm forestry activities, the farmers needed an available and reliable supply of seedlings.[41] The two Khartoum area nurseries, Moghran, controlled by the provincial government, and Soba, controlled by the CFA and the Forestry Research Centre, contained ample land and staff, but provided few seedlings for the public due to shortages in water, nursery materials, and transport. ERC grants were awarded to both nurseries on 15 December 1983.[42]

Neither nursery succeeded in increasing both seedling production and seedling sales and distribution to area farmers. The Soba nursery did not even begin work on renovating its facilities until April 1985, after the ERC threatened to withdraw its grant funds. The Moghran nursery expanded annual seedling production from 40,000 to over 150,000 seedlings in its first year, but it did not manage to transfer many of these to farmers. Most were issued free to local youth groups in a single, bulk transfer that took place in order to rid the seedling beds of overmature seedlings and make room for new plantings. ERC foresters could not find any evidence of the successful planting of any significant amount of the youth groups' seedlings, and it was assumed that most had died.[43] The ERC grant enabled the Moghran nursery to repair one of its small lorries to assist in forestry promotion and seedling sales, and to produce large road signs and other promotional materials to further farmer and public education in the benefits of forestry. However, ERC staff noted that the repaired vehicle was seldom used for these desired activities, and the signs, completed in 1984, by October 1985 still were not erected on nearby roadsides.[44]

*Grant progress and institutional problems*
The ERC had encountered a problem far larger than physical and financial difficulties in its work with the government nurseries. The nurseries had been established to provide seedlings for local CFA and regional government needs, and their work was still devoted to this internal service function. Working with local farmers might be a good idea, but it was not the job of the nursery foresters.

In order for the nurseries to make a greater contribution towards the expansion of forestry on agricultural holdings, a fundamental change in the CFA's policy regarding their roles would have been necessary. To attract and support farmer involvement in forestry, the nurseries needed to adopt a more outward-looking, service-oriented attitude, seeking to become a focal point for initiating local user interaction in forestry technology development for small farms. This sort of institutional innovation might have enabled these Khartoum nurseries to assume the essential role in farm forestry innovation that the ERC and its advisory committee envisioned for them.

## ERC Dissemination Unit Support for Fuelwood/Forestry Activities

The ERC involved the RERI Dissemination Unit in assisting its fuelwood/forestry activities from the unit's own establishment in January 1984.

Initially its work consisted of the publication of studies of forestry issues in the northern and Kordofan regions by advisory committee members, and of two information brochures on tree planting and shelterbelt design.[45] These publications helped increase public awareness of the ERC forestry programme.

As the programme itself progressed and it became evident that the most promising work was occurring in the agricultural scheme forestry and village forestry sectors, the Dissemination Unit (DU) concentrated its efforts on informing and encouraging technology users in these areas. The DU used publications to demonstrate to farmers and villagers that they could play a major role in shaping forestry work in their areas, and that raising trees and planting shelterbelts and woodlots were tasks they could take a lead role in designing and implementing. Workshops and seminars provided more intensive and hands-on introductions to these same topics, and helped in improving contacts between forestry professionals and local farmers and community organizations. These three types of activities are described in more detail below.

*New publications*

The DU's reports on forestry during 1985 centred around the theme of agriculture-forestry integration. Two studies discussed the potential for forestry inclusion in irrigated agriculture, the first for the Khartoum area, and the second for the irrigated sector as a whole.[46] A third study by Derek Earl, described in Chapter 5, examined potential agriculture-forestry interaction on the rainfed schemes of the mechanized farming sector.[47] All reports were circulated to both CFA and agricultural scheme offices throughout the regions where potential projects could be formulated.

The DU also prepared articles for local Arabic and English language newspapers and magazines on ERC forestry activities. These described the novelty of its measures such as initiating village-run nurseries, and agricultural scheme-operated forestry projects.[48]

*Nursery workshop*

The establishment of small village and farm nurseries played an important role in facilitating the institutional changes sought by ERC forestry work, by providing greater control over forestry resource production and utilization to the farmer beneficiaries of SREP grants. Recognizing this, the DU worked with ERC foresters to develop a nursery workshop, in which existing and potential grantees would be trained in nursery establishment and management techniques. The workshop, which took place from 16–21 February 1985, had eleven participants (not including DU and ERC forestry staff), of which five were from ongoing village and farm forestry projects, and one from the Seleit scheme. The other trainees were three members of the Sudan Socialist Union, the country's sole political organization (at that time), with branches in all parts of Sudan, a representative of PLAN

Sudan, an international voluntary organization operating community development projects in the Central region, and a farmer from the Blue Nile province who wished to build his own nursery.[49]

The workshop covered the technical aspects of nursery construction, seedling raising, and seed collection. Talks and practical work also involved forestry matters related to community nursery operation, such as tree identification and species selection, costs and benefits of afforestation in agricultural areas, and seedling transport and transplantation.[50] All participants had a chance to take part in actual seedling preparation and transplanting activities at the Moghran nursery, which hosted the workshop. The DU provided an illustrated manual covering the workshop material and issued certificates of completion to all participants, both of which were handed out by the ERC Director at the closing ceremony.[51]

While it is difficult to assess the actual transfer of knowledge that took place as a result of the workshop, it did succeed in stimulating new interest in village and farm forestry involving nursery establishment. Between February and October 1985 the ERC received grant proposals from the Blue Nile farmer, PLAN Sudan, and the village of Markha Awaj Ed Dareb in Kordofan, whose *sheikh* had been informed of the ERC's programme by colleagues in the Sudan Socialist Union, of which he was a member.[52] The DU planned to continue nursery training in workshops and similar programmes in the future.[53]

*Agriculture-forestry integration seminar*
Encouraged by the success of the Seleit project, the ERC had the DU organize a meeting of senior agriculture and forestry officials from all regions of Sudan to promote similar irrigated scheme forestry projects. The resulting seminar, named ÁFTAH ('open', in Arabic) – Agriculture and Forestry, Towards an Abundant Harvest, took place from 10–13 August 1985, and had some 50 participants, including leading agriculture, forestry, and irrigation specialists from Sudan.[54] Presentations were made by experts from all three fields on how forestry and agriculture could work co-operatively to benefit both crop and wood product interests.

Just as it had benefited from neighbouring country expertise in its charcoal stoves programme, the ERC found its AFTAH efforts greatly assisted by the presence of Dr Hosni El Lakani, an Egyptian forester. ERC foresters had visited agricultural scheme forestry projects in Egypt, where similar environmental and irrigation conditions to those in Sudan prevailed.[55] They were impressed by the degree of commitment to tree growing for shelterbelts and canalside plantings shown by Egyptian farmers, researchers, and government officials, and had recommended that Dr El Lakani attend AFTAH to explain the Egyptian experience to a greater number of Sudanese foresters and agriculturalists.[56]

The AFTAH conference was held in a leading Khartoum hotel and conference centre, with out-of-town participants provided with meals and accommodation. Every effort was made to administer AFTAH according to international conference standards, to demonstrate the ERC's regard for the importance and potential of work in this area. Several of the invited experts were asked to prepare papers, which were circulated to all participants and discussed during the seminar sessions. ERC reports and promotional materials on agriculture-forestry integration were also circulated to the participants.

AFTAH revealed institutional friction between foresters and agriculturalists as well as opportunities for more positive interaction. During the proceedings some foresters criticized the agricultural schemes for causing environmental damage through deforestation, and agriculturalists criticized foresters for promoting tree planting in areas where this could attract destructive birds, and cause canal seepage and other hazards.[57] The ERC hoped that this public airing of grievances would enable the two groups of professionals to resolve past differences and to work towards a new relationship that recognized each others' concerns.

The participants visited the Seleit project to observe how the AFTAH ideals could work in practice, with the Seleit director (and not ERC foresters) guiding the tour and explaining all activities. On the last day of the conference, the ERC Director talked about the SREP grants programme, suggesting that proposals for work in a similar vein would be favourably received by the Technical Committee. He stressed that the ERC wished to receive proposals not from forestry authorities, but from the schemes themselves, with local foresters enlisted in service to the larger agricultural activities.[58] This would insure that the agriculturalists would play an active role in the new technology development, and it would encourage the movement of forestry personnel into a more interactive and service-orientated role with these technology users.

Within four months of the end of the AFTAH seminar, seven large agricultural schemes applied for and received SREP grants to initiate or expand forestry activities on their lands.[59] The ERC brought two new foresters onto its staff to assist in the support and monitoring of its rapidly expanding work in this area.[60] As has been mentioned previously, the CFA acting director pledged his full support in providing foresters from his staff to support the schemes in their new grant projects. Thus, the institutional innovation that underlay the success of the Seleit project was in the process of dissemination throughout the irrigated agricultural sector.

## Institutional Innovation and Increased User Participation

The ERC fuelwood/forestry programme was not founded on the technical aspects of the forestry technology it sought to promote. Neither the species nor the methods it employed were new either to forestry science or to the Sudan. However, the most successful projects it supported through SREP grants all involved an innovation in the relationship between forestry and

124

agricultural authorities, whether on the large scheme or village levels – innovation that put technology users in a more prominent role in technology development activities.

In the ERC's work with large, irrigated agricultural schemes, SREP grant-based projects put foresters directly under the authority and direction of agricultural managers, as opposed to previous work that segregated lands and authority into agricultural and forestry spheres. In the village forestry area, SREP grants, through putting funds directly into the hands of village authorities, gave those authorities a new control over forestry measures that inspired them to devise (with technical assistance from ERC foresters) and advance afforestation measures even under the most adverse physical circumstances. Even in the generally poorer-performing grant project areas of farm forestry and government nursery support, those individual projects in which farmers acquired the greatest responsibility for seedling production and plantation design, and in which foresters adopted a less-dominating, more advisory role, made the greatest progress.

The more innovation involved in the relationship between foresters and local technology users in SREP grant projects, the more those projects achieved innovation in forestry development in their areas of Sudan. When users were allowed to determine the types of forestry practices they wished to implement, and the location and manner in which these practices would be implemented, they responded with a greater participation in and commitment to the successful implementation of their projects.

The forestry work the ERC has initiated has significant potential for forest resource development in Sudan, if it can be replicated on a larger scale. The incorporation of forestry programmes into irrigated agriculture scheme design holds particular promise. It has been estimated that, by planting trees on canal banks, marginal lands, and 5 per cent of present agricultural lands (in the form of shelterbelts and border plantings) within the irrigated sector, over 30 per cent of urban fuelwood demand and over 10 per cent of total fuelwood demand in central Sudan could be provided for on a sustained yield basis.[61] At the same time, the positive environmental changes that accompany afforestation, shelter from hot, drying winds and increased moisture retention, could lead to improved crop performance. The Egyptian experience with shelterbelt plantings has demonstrated such beneficial effects.[62]

The main obstacle to achieving such goals is not technical capability; it is institutional isolation and rigidity. Sudanese forestry authorities need to re-integrate their work into general agricultural development efforts, and seek to get local technology users involved in forestry technology development efforts.

# Innovation and Forest Energy Development: Wider Institutional Implications of the Sudanese Experience

Participation . . . helps ready people for change by giving them a broader outlook and more skills . . . participative teams are not equivalent to 'groupthink', or inaction without consensus, or management by committee. . . . They are action bodies that develop better systems, methods, products, or policies than would result from unilateral action by one responsible segment, or even from each of the team members working in isolation from the others. The results are likely to be more innovative and more easily used.[1]

The above passage is a fitting summary of the experiences cited in the previous chapters concerning forest energy development in Sudan. Yet, it was not written about Sudan, nor was it written about forestry, about energy, or even about a development issue. The passage comes from Rosabeth Moss Kanter's book on how American industrial management should change in order to meet the challenge of remaining competitive in the technology-dominated markets of the future.

The aptness of Kanter's words in the context of this book illustrates its central tenet: that innovation, whether in high-technology industry or a poor rural village, thrives on the exploitation of knowledge of both technical possibility and existing demand. Encouraging the participation of technology users in the R & D process increases the likelihood that its products will profit from user knowledge and skill, and in so doing achieve widespread and successful application in the field. User-orientated and user-involved R & D possesses the awareness and the flexibility needed to cope with the variations, national, regional, and local, in conditions and demands in formulating robust designs and in re-innovating those designs as the innovation's environment itself evolves over time. The ERC's experience in Sudan demonstrates the importance of responding to such variations, whether through adjusting stove or forestry technologies to accommodate local needs, or through restructuring an entire technology development programme to acknowledge indigenous skills and resources, as in the case of charcoal production. Peters and Waterman, in seeking the sources of industrial success in America in their popular and influential work, *In Search of Excellence*, stressed the importance of this same awareness and responsiveness:

innovative companies not only are unusually good at producing commercially viable new widgets; *innovative companies are especially adroit at continually responding to change of any sort in their environments* [emphasis theirs].[2]

## Implications for Renewable Energy organizations

The energy field, in general, has tended to work in a more isolated manner than other professions on technology development. Energy work as a whole, and forest energy work as a part of this whole, has been pervaded with an invention, supply-orientated bias which, crudely put, expresses the sentiment that, if fuel and machines to use it are provided, all development problems will be solved. This bias has led to the work attitude that, if enough time is spent in the laboratory designing and testing hardware, the needed machines and fuel will emerge, and that all that scientists and engineers require from outside the laboratory is basic information on resource availability and cost, so that they can calculate the cost per unit of energy output of their R & D products.

This bias has given scant attention to both user needs and the potential contribution of users to the innovation process. As is noted in Chapter 3, recent evaluations of renewable energy efforts have singled out this neglect as a prime cause of poor innovation performance. The Sudanese experience demonstrates that strategies that encourage users to participate in forest energy technology development lead to successful innovation. Work in forest energy, as well as work in renewable energy in general, needs to follow the movements in more mature development fields, such as agriculture, irrigation, and public health, and make its R & D system more user-interactive. It should not de-emphasize or curtail the contributions of scientists and engineers to technology development, but it should complement and enhance these efforts by incorporating the knowledge and skills of technology users into the design and dissemination process.

Forest energy development, in particular, depends strongly on responsiveness to environmental conditions. Its technologies must be sensitive to ecological capacities and constraints, which can vary substantially from location to location. Without the benefit of local knowledge of these conditions, it is difficult to see how such technologies can hope to be implemented over a wide area. Richards's comments on the implications of environmental variability for agricultural development efforts apply with equal weight to work in the forest energy sector:

> many environmental problems are, in fact, localized and specific, and require local, ecologically particular responses. One of the answers ... is through mobilizing and building upon existing local skills and initiatives. Everything should be done ... to stimulate vigorous 'indigenous science' and 'indigenous technology'.[3]

It now seems that, at least in the forestry area of forest energy development, the importance of the user role is beginning to be recognized. A recent FAO publication states at its outset,

> the scope and widespread dispersion of rural needs for local tree cover is now so great that it can only be tackled in an essentially self-help fashion

by the people themselves . . . rural forestry innovations must be based on an understanding of traditional tree management practices and indigenous knowledge, of both men and women.[4]

While one might dispute that local needs and assistance capacities are any more diverse and less powerful, respectively, at present than they were at any point in the past, and question why the FAO chooses today, rather than ten years ago, to make such a statement, it is encouraging to see this sort of sentiment expressed by a major actor in forest energy development assistance. The FAO document also cites user involvement as the key to successful innovation in forestry activities:

> Innovations should never be construed as replacements for existing indigenous means of building upon local strength and capabilities. Effective design and introduction of forestry innovations ultimately require an understanding of where these activities fall within the spectrum of people's [sic] spontaneous responses to scarcity. This will only come with direct two-way communication between project planners and rural people, and a collaborative effort to devise methods by which the most appropriate innovations might be effectively introduced.[5]

One can only hope that this recognition will come to be shared not only by other donors in the forestry field, but also by all those engaged in other aspects of forest energy technology development, whether their focus is upon stove improvement, charcoal production, or the myriad of other fuels and devices based upon the utilization of forest resources.

*Implications for government R & D management*

The ERC, as it transformed itself to become more aware of and amenable to user contributions in technology development, achieved its first successes in moving technologies from the laboratory to the field, factory and farm. Institutional structure and human resource management thus stand out as important factors in innovation in forest energy development. These management factors, cited by Kanter and others in Chapter 2 as important to the maintenance of competitive advantage in an industrial situation, have equal application within the context of technology and development. Building internal capacity to encourage and nurture new ideas, whether they come from inside or outside an organization, is a cornerstone of sound innovation management.

The ERC, in encouraging its staff to work directly with users on technology development matters, and through promoting user-interactive R & D through the work of its Dissemination Unit, transformed its basic institutional structure into a form more conducive to innovation. In so doing, the organization moved towards the formation of the 'organic' linkages between government R & D and technology users espoused by Norman Clark. Rather than strengthening the barriers of hierarchy that can isolate R & D groups from the productive sectors of the economy, the ERC sought to dismantle such barriers and increase its ties to technology users.

In so doing, it moved towards Clark's 'biological model' for institutional behaviour in the management of technical change.

*Implications for development assistance*

At the development assistance level, the challenge is how to channel the resources of developed nations into supporting the transformation of technology development work and the local institutions supporting that work into a more interactive, user-orientated framework. The chapters concerned with forest energy development in Sudan contained little mention of the US Agency for International Development and its specific actions in relation to the implementation of any of the technology development programmes of the ERC. This omission does not reflect a failure on USAID's part, but rather one of the most successful elements of its SREP project. While it provided critical financial resources to support the ERC's activities, USAID left the fundamental decisions about technology directions and project implementation to the Sudanese institution. The long-term technical advisors from the Georgia Institute of Technology helped to set up the REDG programme and other management systems within the ERC, but the ERC Technical Committee alone decided on all grant applications, and also approved all consultancy arrangements. ERC staff also maintained the responsibility for monitoring and evaluating all grant activities.

In this way, the development assistance offered to the ERC concentrated less upon meeting specific technology production outputs than it did on developing indigenous expertise in managing technology development and innovations. SREP's importance lies less in the particular kilns, stoves, or trees that it supported, than in the manner in which it undertook their development. By centering the project about the REDG programme, which required the ERC to both establish links with external technology users, and to refine its own structure to accept and respond to user inputs, USAID encouraged the organization to interact with users in its technology development efforts. USAID provided an incentive for institutional innovations with the ERC itself, to make the organization more open to the contributions from local knowledge and skill resources.

Development assistance in forest energy in other nations can profit from this example. More emphasis should be placed on management skills, not in the sense of MBA degrees, but rather in respect to abilities to communicate, evaluate, and make decisions, however these may be obtained. While specialized skills in various scientific disciplines, commonly obtained through the pursuit of diplomas and degrees, are important aids to the management of technical change, excessive specialization can be counterproductive, if it leads to a tendency to dismiss potential contributions to technical change that originate from outside research facilities.[6] Development assistance appears, in the energy area, to have over-specialized and under-communicated, producing institutions and projects dominated by often inappropriate and impractical technical concerns. This balance should be redressed by stressing the importance of interactive R & D, and using training to provide the skills necessary for developing country professionals to carry out such work.

Kanter, in assessing the task of restoring America's global competitiveness, remarks,

the problem before us is not to invent more tools, but to use the ones we have.[7]

Using available resources should be considered the central task for development assistance. Unfortunately, too much assistance focuses on invention, neglecting this more important concern of innovation. This balance needs to be redressed. The utilization of existing resources, in the form of incorporating user participation into forest energy development programmes, provides both the problem and the solution for assistance in generating new technologies and applying them towards innovation in developing nations.

# Notes

## Chapter 1

**1** Joseph Schumpeter, 'The Analysis of Economic Change,' *The Review of Economic Statistics* (May 1935), p 7, quoted in Nathan Rosenberg, p 6.
**2** This distinction between invention and innovation is indebted to Freeman's discussion of this topic, Chapter 5.
**3** R. Rothwell and P. Gardiner (1985), p 168.
**4** Von Hippel tends towards the narrower definition of 'user', with Rothwell and Gardiner employing a more general notion. More discussion of this point is found in Chapter 2.
**5** See Cohen and Uphoff, pp 213–236.

## Chapter 2

**1** Amilcar O Herrera p 27.
**2** Adam Smith, p 11.
**3** Marx and Engels, p 83. The author is indebted to Christopher Freeman for calling his attention to this quotation. See Freeman, p 105.
**4** The concept of technology being treated as a 'black box' phenomenon was originated by Nathan Rosenberg, who later published a series of his essays on this theme titled *Inside the Black Box: Technology and Economics*. Christopher Freeman, another seminal figure in the economics of technical change, echoes Rosenberg's view of the inadequate treatment economists have given technology: 'although most economists have made a deferential nod in the direction of technical change, few have stopped to examine it.' See Freeman, p 4.
**5** Freeman, p 109.
**6** Langrish *et al*, pp 73–75. This report on a survey of the Queens Award-winning innovations was the first to use this terminology (with 'demand-pull', 'science-push', and 'technology-push' substituted for Langrish's original phrases in some later studies. In this early entrant to the push-pull debate, it was argued that most of the innovations surveyed were of the 'demand-pull' type, but that the larger technological changes tended to be of the 'discovery-push' type. This book does not go into a lengthy discussion of work in this area, but a good review of some of the major case studies can be found in David Mowery and Nathan Rosenberg, 'The Influence of Market Demand Upon Innovation: A Critical Review of Some Empirical Studies,' in Rosenberg, pp 193–241.
**7** An excellent analysis of hovercraft's development can be found in Roy Rothwell and Paul Gardiner (1985), pp 167–186.
**8** See Brian Shaw, pp 283–92.
**9** Mowery and Rosenberg, pp 230–231.
**10** *Ibid*, p 230.
**11** Freeman, p 169.

**12** Adam Smith, p 13.

**13** Eric A Von Hippel (January 1978), p. 31. Others now writing about user innovation include Holt (August 1985), pp 199–208; and Yao Tsu Li and Blais (August 1982), pp 255–273.

**14** *Ibid*, p 34. It is worth noting that Von Hippel is now consolidating much of the work of his research group in a forthcoming book, *User, Manufacturer, and Supplier Innovation: An Analysis of the Functional Sources of Innovation* (Sloan School of Management, Cambridge, Massachusetts).

**15** Von Hippel (March–April 1982), pp 117–118.

**16** *Ibid*, p 118.

**17** *Ibid*, pp 226–234.

**18** The study of the design process is a growing concern in the field of innovation analysis. A compilation of some of the most useful work in this area is found in Roy and Wield.

**19** Gardiner and Rothwell (January 1985), p 7.

**20** *Ibid*, p 17.

**21** For more details, see Rothwell and Gardiner (August 1985), pp 167–186.

**22** R M Bell p 41.

**23** *Ibid*, p. 38.

**24** The reader is referred to two useful collections of literature in this area: Stewart and James; and Fransman and King.

**25** Fransman, 'Technological Capability in the Third World,' in Fransman and King, eds, p 4.

**26** *Ibid*, pp 5–6.

**27** *Ibid*, p 6.

**28** E F Schumacher, pp 175, 177.

**29** *Ibid*, p 18.

**30** Whitcombe and Carr p 55.

**31** There are many interesting works in these two areas, only a few of which can be discussed in any detail in this work. Important works on ITK include: David Brokensha *et al*; Harwood; Korten *et al*; and all the articles in *IDS Bulletin* (January 1979), edited by Michael Howes and Robert Chambers. Significant works on ISP include: articles in *World Development* (September–October 1978), devoted entirely to a discussion of the urban informal sector; Teriba and Kayode, especially chapters by Harris, Harris and Rowe, and Schatz; Mead, pp 1095–1106; Odufalu, pp 593–607; Page, pp 159–182; Keith Hart, pp 61–90; Marris and Somerset; Steel. See bibliography for more details on specific articles that the author has found particularly useful.

**32** Biggs, pp 23–26.

**33** Sansom, pp 109–121.

**34** Brammer, pp 24–28.

**35** King, pp 92–140.

**36** For examples of this local innovation, see *ibid*, pp 44–65, and Hart, p 84.

**37** The author is indebted to Robert Chambers for introducing him to much of the work in this area, and to the informative paper by Chambers and Jiggins. However, any errors in the representation of the research discussed in this section are the sole responsibility of the author.

**38** Rhoades pp 139–150.

**39** Ashby (1984).

**40** Richards (1985), pp 71–72.

**41** See Belshaw, pp 24–27.

**42** Richards, p 72.

**43** See Matlon *et al*.

**44** See WHO and UNICEF (1978), p 5.

**45** Quoted in Bannerman *et al* (1983), pp 7–8.

**46** See *ibid*.

**47** See, for example: Folch-Lyon *et al*, Schearer and Suyono *et al*, all found in *Studies in Family Planning* (December 1981), pp 409–432, 407–408, and 433–442, respectively.

**48** Ruttan, p 42.

**49** See Lowdermilk, pp 2–7.

**50** Some of Allen's original ideas are contained in *Industrial Management Review* (Fall 1966), pp 87–98. A compilation of much of his work is found in his *Managing the Flow of Technology* (1977).

**51** Allen (1977), pp 249–265.

**52** Rogers and Shoemaker, pp 183–185.

**53** *Ibid*, pp 200–224.

**54** Barnett, Bell, and Hoffman p 175.

**5̈** Rogers, p 220. In this and another article in the same volume ('The Passing of the Dominant Paradigm – Reflections on Diffusion Research,' pp 49–52), Rogers voices his doubts about the fixed, mechanistic approach to diffusion research that has developed, and agrees with a statement by a Dean of a US communications school that, in this sense, the diffusion field has been 'a mile wide and an inch deep' (p 219). Although Rogers urges a more time-series approach to remedy some of the field's methodological problems, his work still suffers from the supposition that users do not play much of a role in the development of technologies. A thought-provoking critique of this aspect of Rogers' work by Syed A Rahim appears in the same volume: 'Diffusion Research – Past, Present, and Future.' pp 223–225.

**56** Nelson and Winter, p 4.

**57** *Ibid*, pp 9–10.

**58** See Kline, pp 36–45.

**59** Clark, p 250.

**60** Kanter, p 19.

**61** Shanklin and Ryans, p 171. A new work making similar points is Bonnet (April 1986), pp 117–126.

**62** Gardiner and Rothwell, p 88.

**63** *Ibid*, p 91.

**64** Clark, p 199.

**65** For a more detailed discussion of such problems, see *ibid*, pp 198–201.

**66** Herrera, p 26.

**67** Clark, pp 201–203.

**68** *Ibid*, p 203.

**69** For a more extensive discussion on this theme, see Jantsch. Norman Clark and Calestous Juma of the Science Policy Research Unit, University of Sussex, are preparing a major work on evolutionary technical change at the time of this writing.

**70** Black, p 7. A more recent work describing the importance of R & D – production sector linkages in innovation is Shekhar Chaudhuri's description of the Swaraj tractor development in India (April 1986), pp 89–103.

**71** MacKerron and Thomas, p 11.

**72** *Ibid*, p 11.

**73** *Ibid*, p 12.

## Chapter 3

**1** US Agency for International Development (12 April 1985), p iii.

**2** An excellent bibliography of works on socio-economic constraints to renewable energy development is found in Barnett, Bell and Hoffman, pp 78–211. For a somewhat updated discussion of socio-economic issues in the forest energy area, and an expanded bibliography, see Agarwal (1986).

**3** Barnett (December 1985).

**4** US Agency for International Development (21 February 1986), p 1.

**5** See Conahan (13 August 1982).

**6** US General Accounting Office (13 August 1982), p 6.

**7** USAID, Bureau for Africa (April 1984, April 1985 and February 1986).

**8** US General Accounting Office, p 2.

**9** *Ibid*, p 5.

**10** USAID, Bureau for Africa, April 1984, p vi.

**11** USAID, The Inspector General, p 22.

**12** USAID, Bureau for Africa, April 1984, p x.

**13** *Ibid*, pp x–xi.

**14** USAID, The Inspector General, p 14.

**15** *Ibid*, p ii.

**16** *Ibid*, pp 13–14.

**17** *Ibid*, p 28.

**18** *Ibid*, p 29.

**19** USAID, Bureau for Asia, p i.

**20** *Ibid*, p 1–1.

**21** USAID, The Inspector General, p 28.

**22** *Ibid*, p 4.

**23** USAID, Bureau for Asia, p 2.6.

**24** For good examples of such sound technical work, with limited attention paid to socio-economic factors, see National Academy of Sciences (1981), pp 95–100, and Earl (1975).

**25** Foley (1986), p 23.

**26** See FAO, *Simple Technologies for Charcoal Making*, for a good example of this sort of newer study.

**27** Agarwal (1986), pp 177–178. Similar comments were made in the earlier work of Barnett, Bell and Hoffman.

**28** Foley, p 23.

**29** This point has been made in Foley, p 15, and Agarwal (1986), pp 178–180.

**30** Personal communications, Tony Prior, USAID Regional Energy Advisor, East Africa, and Tony Paddon, Tropical Products Development Centre (consultant to improved charcoal production project, Somalia).

**31** Powell in Brown (1978), pp 115–128.

**32** Often the moisture content of the wood input is not taken into consideration, so that the actual energy input cannot be assessed. In other cases, volume measures are used, leaving even greater confusion as to the actual energy inputs and outputs of the charcoal conversion process. For more explanation of these and other problems in charcoal conversion measurement, see Foley, pp 83–84. Chapter 5 contains a discussion of the specific measurement problems that faced the Energy Research Council's work on charcoal production in Sudan.

**33** French, p 26. French's investigations into local charcoal manufacture are described on pp 25–26.

**34** Foley, p 20.

**35** *Ibid*, p 15.

**36** Foley and Moss, p 18.

**37** For further references on improved stoves work, see Foley and Moss; Agarwal (1986), and Pereira in Bhatia and Pereira, Chapter 8. For more primary material on ongoing stoves projects, see *Boiling Point*, the monthly stoves journal of the Intermediate Technology Development Group, Rugby, UK.

**38** For good articulations of these questions, see Hoskins, and Joseph and Hassrick.

**39** Foley and Moss, p 13.

**40** See Pereira, pp 8.2–8.11 for more detailed discussion of these needs and how they influence adoption decisions.

**41** See Clarke.

**42** Prasad in Clarke, p 2.

**43** See, in Clarke: Diop; Ki-Zerbo; Makuria; Navaratna; Krishna Prasad; Sarin; Soumare and Sudjarwo. Note that this does not represent a complete list of the case studies presented, as those which take a different view of the task of innovation are discussed in more detail later in the text.

**44** Massé, p 26.

**45** Khosla, pp 91–92.

**46** Kinyanjui, pp 150–157.

**47** See G P W Scoble, pp 50–58.

**48** Joseph, Shanahan, and Stewart, p 19. The ITDG stove project staff, it should be said, have been practising their work far better than they have been writing about it, and the criticisms of their illustration should not be taken as fundamental criticisms of their work efforts in the field.

**49** Agarwal (1986), p 168.

**50** For a good general introduction to the field of agroforestry, see Douglas and Hart.

**51** For a compilation of the types of issues that arose, and examples of such, see DEVRES (1980).

**52** In recognition of the importance of socio-economic factors in forestry development, the World Bank, a major donor in the forestry area, supported two studies of this topic (1980 and 1981). Another useful work on social obstacles to forestry is Skutsch.

**53** FAO (24–28 June), p 3. The experts at this meeting deleted a similar phrase from the meeting report during the final plenary session, finding it too harsh, but included 'Common strategies and tactics in implementing arid zone forestry policies that have been successful are rare', FAO (24–28 June), p 26.

**54** Catterson, Gulick, and Resch, p 1.

**55** US Agency for International Development (August 1984), p B5.

**56** *Ibid*, p B6.

**57** Lindberg and Hobgood, pp 1–2.

**58** See Bandyopedhyay, pp 1, 6; and Hall and Percy.

**59** See Mahiti Team.

**60** World Bank (26 January 1983), p 2.

**61** FAO, 'Policy, Institutions, and Socio-Economic Considerations,' p 5.

**62** FAO, 'Summary Report, Expert Consultation on the Role of Forestry in Combatting Desertification,' p 7.

**63** Catterson *et al*, p 6.

**64** *Ibid*, p 11.

**65** FAO, 'Policy, Institutions, and Socio-Economic Considerations,' p 11.

**66** *Ibid*, p 5.

**67** *Ibid*, p 7.

**68** Two publications marked the outset of this new community forestry effort: FAO, *Forestry for Local Community Development* (Rome: FAO, 1978); and FAO, *Forestry for Rural Communities* (Rome: FAO, 1978). The former document was more technical in nature, the latter more political and policy-orientated.

**69** FAO (Rome: FAO, 1981).

**70** FAO (Rome: FAO, 1985).

# Chapter 4

**1** This and the following energy demand statistics taken from National Energy Administration/Ministry of Energy and Mining (March 1983), pp 3–10.

2 NEA, *Annex 1*, p 90.

3 *Ibid*, pp 90–93.

4 The positive-feedback state of deforestation in sub-Saharan Africa is best described in a recent publication by the Worldwatch Institute (1985).

5 For more details, see Chapter 5 and Gaafar El Faki Ali (August 1985).

6 Little information is available on income from this ubiquitous but poorly monitored trade, but its importance has been emphasized in personal conversations with Gaafar El Faki Ali and Hamza Homoudi, the senior foresters in the ERC. Also, the presence of these products in small markets found in every area of population concentration in Sudan visited by the author attests to the demand for these products.

7 Prices recorded by author: LS 1.8 = $1 in 1982 and it is difficult to calculate the real increase in the price of charcoal during this time, as Sudan has no reliable figures on cost of living or inflation for this period, and many basic commodities, such as bread and sugar, are under government subsidies and fixed prices. However, the success of the ERC's introduction of charcoal-saving new stoves designs, described in Chapter 6, attests to consumer awareness of the rising costs of this domestic fuel.

8 UNESCO (Paris: UNESCO, 1985), Table, 3.12.

9 World Bank (16 April 1986), p. iv.

10 This status was removed by the Transitional Military Government that took power upon the overthrow of the Nimeri regime in April 1985. However the NCR Director still maintains a prominent role on national committees, consisting of himself and senior ministers, dealing with scientific and natural resources issues.

11 The following discussion is heavily indebted to M Alassam, pp 3–11.

12 His intention to re-centralize the administration of forestry affairs was made clear in a public announcement by His Excellency Siddig Abdin, Minister of Agriculture, in his keynote address to the ERC's AFTAH Conference, 10 August 1985, recorded in Mary Clarkin (October 1985), pp 12–13.

13 Amal Tijani Ali, p 3.

14 The author is indebted to Dr El Tayeb Idris Eisa, Director, Energy Research Council, for providing this informaton on the history of the NCR and its component bodies. The comments on the political elements of this history, however, reflect the authors individual opinion based on his direct experience with the parties involved and are his responsibility alone.

15 See Lillywhite and Lillywhite.

16 Georgia Institute of Technology (February 1982), pp 1–2.

17 USAID feelings in this regard are recorded in the author's notes on the initial meeting between USAID officials and the technical assistance staff from the Georgia Institute of Technology on 27 November 1982. See author's journal, 27 November 1982. The motivation behind USAID's change of view regarding the design and implementation of renewable energy projects was discussed in Chapter 3.

18 Additional foresters were added to the Dissemination Unit staff later in the project, as the large number of grants awarded in this technology area necessitated the expansion of ERC assistance and monitoring personnel.

19 See USAID/Government of Sudan (31 August 1981). The official exchange value for Sudanese pounds at this time was $1 = LS 0.81.

20 The nature of the REDG programme remained somewhat unclear to the Sudanese, and the requirement that grant funds be awarded to parties outside of the ERC had to be clarified at a meeting of senior USAID and GOS officials on 7 November 1983. This meeting is discussed in greater detail in Chapter 6.

21 The listed technologies are noted in Georgia Institute of Technology, *Proposal for Sudan Rural Renewable Energy Project*, p 19.

**22** The wood stoves area was later redefined to focus upon industrial woodfuels consumption technologies.

## Chapter 5

**1** National Energy Administration/Ministry of Energy and Mining, *Sudan National Energy Assessment: Annex 1*, p 5.
**2** *Ibid*, p 107.
**3** *Ibid*, p 92.
**4** *Ibid*, p 17.
**5** This assumes an energy equivalence of 30 MJ/kg charcoal, and 18 MJ/kg firewood.
**6** See Sudan Renewable Energy Project (29 November 1983).
**7** See Hassan Osman Abd El Nour (February 1984), pp 39–40.
**8** *Ibid*, p 39, and National Energy Administration, *Sudan National Energy Assessment: Annex 1*, p 90. It is interesting to note that the NEA recorded Jackson's reservations; but although its staff did endeavour to revise growing stock estimates in its Energy Assessment, they did not query conversion efficiency estimates. Abd El Nour also points out that Saini, in using Jackson's ratio, noted that it was only a crude measure, with great potential error.
**9** See Abd El Nour in Earl pp 39–40.
**10** National Energy Administration, *Sudan National Energy Assessment: Annex 1*, p 17.
**11** Abd El Nour in Earl p 48.
**12** *Ibid*, pp 49–50.
**13** *Ibid*, p 17.
**14** *Ibid*, pp 17–19 and p 52.
**15** *Ibid*, p 12.
**16** *Ibid*, p 12.
**17** See Abd El Nour and Satti, p 24.
**18** *Ibid*, p 35.
**19** *Ibid*, p 32.
**20** *Ibid*, p 3.
**21** See Sudan Renewable Energy Project (31 May 1984), p 22.
**22** Abd El Nour and Satti, p 2.
**23** *Ibid*, p 1.
**24** See Satti and Dorré, pp 3–4.
**25** *Ibid*, pp 6–11.
**26** *Ibid*, pp 14–16. One small element of extrapolation did exist in the Satti and Dorré study. They analyzed the contents of sample charcoal sacks, noting the presence of brands, fines, and other impurities. In assessing overall conversion efficiency, they reduced total charcoal output by extrapolating these weights, and the weights of the sacks themselves, over the total number of sacks, and deducting this figure from total sack output. This enabled their resulting conversion figure, they argued, to reflect the amount of usable charcoal produced per unit of wood carbonized, rather than a less specific measure of total kiln output per fuelwood input. The deduction of estimated brands, fines, and impurities from measured kiln outputs served to reduce the net conversion efficiency calculation, so this extrapolation in no way detracted from the veracity of their high conversion efficiency findings.
**27** FAO, *Simple Technologies for Charcoal Making*, notes that a conversion ratio of 4 tonnes wood input: tonne charcoal output is obtained in efficient earth, brick, and metal kiln designs. By this standard, the 3.4:1 ratio obtained in Sudanese earth kilns indicates high efficiency.

**28** Satti and Dorré, p 5.

**29** *Ibid*, p 1.

**30** Ali. While his work was not finished until August 1985, the main findings were available to the ERC from late 1984, at which time it began an extensive revision of its implementation plan for the charcoal production area.

**31** See *Ibid*, pp II–III.

**32** *Ibid*, p 31.

**33** *Ibid*, p 31.

**34** *Ibid*, p III.

**35** *Ibid*, p 2.

**36** *Ibid*, p 6.

**37** *Ibid*, p 12.

**38** *Ibid*, p 7.

**39** See Sudan Renewable Energy Project (May 1985), p 11.

**40** Adrian Vinke, Forest Management Expert, FAO, Sudan, personal communication.

**41** See Earl (April 1985).

**42** *Ibid*, pp 26–28.

**43** *Ibid*, pp 26–27.

**44** *Ibid*, pp 29–30.

**45** *Ibid*, pp 38–39.

**46** *Ibid*, pp 34–58. Earl undertakes a detailed economic analysis of the costs and benefits of charcoal making operations for each company in this work.

**47** Grant applications received 28 April and 5 May 1985, respectively; awards of LS 12,760 and LS 12,000 made on 30 May 1985.

**48.** The author is indebted to Keith Openshaw and Derek Earl, who separately pointed out this discrepancy. Nothing has been published on this matter, nor has the NEA sought to clarify the figures.

**49** National Energy Administration, *Sudan National Energy Assessment: Annex 1*, p 92.

**50** See Earl (February 1984), p 21; and Mukhtar cited in *ibid*, p 21. Both Earl and Mukhtar made generous allowances for illegal, unrecorded charcoal production in their calculations, with Earl assuming that 90 per cent of total production went unrecorded, and Mukhtar assuming 92 per cent. In spite of these allowances, their production estimates were little more than 20 per cent of the figure produced by the NEA from extrapolations upon household consumption survey results.

**51** National Energy Administration, *Sudan National Energy Assessment: Annex 1*, note (3), Table IV–20, p 92.

# Chapter 6

**1** These projects included now defunct work on improved stoves by the Sudan Council of Churches in the Nile Province, and by Norwegian Church Aid in Equatoria; and ongoing efforts by CARE, in Kordofan, and ACORD, in Equatoria. The CARE and ACORD projects are discussed in greater detail later in the text. As stated in the text, none of the above programmes succeeded in establishing independent production and distribution of new stove designs before the initiation of SREP's stove programme.

**2** See Nasr El Din, p 2.

**3** *Ibid*, p 2.

**4** Ahfad's founders were especially concerned about female circumcision in Sudan, a widespread and growing practice that was regarded as one of the major sources of female health problems. They hoped that the college would provide a forum where such matters could be discussed openly and frankly, without the pressures and prejudices of family members and neighbours. The college later broadened its curriculum to include such subjects as home economics, nutrition, psychology and child development.

**5** Nasr El Din, p 2.

**6** Nor did the ERC ask these questions in subsequent field trials, although, in retrospect, they probably could have provided useful information. Since the author's departure from Sudan, the ERC has undertaken extensive new field survey work, in order to obtain more ideas from household users on how the stoves programme can be improved. These new studies were the result of recommendations of the consultancy on charcoal stoves marketing, to be discussed later in this chapter.

**7** Author's own notes, based on conversations with Nasr El Din and Majoub about the methodology of their field research in their 1980 and 1983 studies. To be fair to them and the Ahfad/University of Khartoum stoves programme, their methodological problems were shared by other renewable energy studies undertaken at that time. The ERC and University researchers were well trained in the technical aspects of the technologies they studied, but received little training in survey technique, or in the general social and economic background of their work.

**8** In one conversation involving the author, a representative of GIT, and other project staff, a professor from the University of Khartoum stated that people without engineering PhD's were not qualified to pursue work on stove improvement. To be fair, such professional elitism was the norm, rather than the exception, among Sudan's senior academics and civil servants.

**9** It was only much later in the development of the stoves programme that any Sudanese women became directly involved in stove construction. The desire of Mary Clarkin, a woman Peace Corps volunteer, to make stoves, and her participation in an SREP producer training workshop, encouraged other women SREP staff to take up hammers and tin snips and to participate in this part of the project.

**10** The international standards are those contained in the testing methods described in VITA, *Testing the Efficiency of Wood-Burning Cookstoves: Provisional International Standards* (Arlington, VA: VITA, 1983). The ERC programme did not follow these standards, although it possessed the VITA publication, for several reasons. Its immediate need was to determine whether the University of Khartoum new stove design was thermodynamically superior to traditional stove designs. A perfectly sound experimental technique to measure efficiency had been developed by the University, and switching to the VITA methods, particularly multiple-test system (involving actual meal preparation and home trials), would have taken much additional time and training. Also, although the VITA methods required only simple laboratory equipment, some of this equipment was not readily obtainable in Sudan. Considering these factors, the ERC decided to continue using its old test methods, and to adopt the VITA procedures at a later date.

**11** In any case, the ERC's efficiency measures from its experimental method averaged 24.5 per cent, and subsequent measurements using VITA international procedures at Kenyatta University, Nairobi, gave an average efficiency of 24.1 per cent, an insignificant difference. See Maxwell Kinyanjui, *Consultant's Report on SREP Charcoal Stoves* (Kenya: Energy/Development International, May 1984), p 4.

**12** See Fadia Majoub, and Ali and Huff, p 6.

**13** Such problems included seasonal fluctuations in demand, multiple sources of supply (several household members gathering or, in this case, buying fuel, or gifts from neighbours), various end uses (cooking, ironing, washing), and physical difficulties in precisely weighing fuel used. A useful discussion of these methodological issues is found in Michael Howes, pp 118–130.

139

**14** Some stoves suffered from broken pot supports, caused by poor spot welding where these were joined to the charcoal holder, and others were not properly assembled, so that attaching and removing the charcoal holder from the main stove body (for loading and cleaning) was difficult.

**15** One researcher quit the project midway through the field trial, and the remaining Ahfad women had to cover her survey area as best they could to complete the data collection.

**16** In the end, only a tiny fraction of the information collected, that concerning consumption figures, was tabulated, with much other information filed away, as staff turned to new technology development issues. No extensive report on the field test was ever completed. This was unfortunate, but the discontinuation of this work freed staff to play important roles in technology promotion and dissemination operations. Descriptions of the field test and some of its data can be found in Nasr El Din, *Improved Charcoal Stove Project*, and Ali and Huff, pp 7–10.

**17** Ali and Huff, p 9.

**18** Author's journal, 1 December 1983.

**19** See Hyman for a good general description of this programme. In the author's opinion, Hyman's article gives insufficient credit to data and observations provided by the staff of the Kenya Renewable Energy Development Project, which administers the stoves programme.

**20** Ali and Huff, p 12.

**21** See Kinyangui (May, 1984), p 7.

**22** The general strategy of this dissemination effort is found in Ali and Gamser (11 April 1984).

**23** Ali and Huff, p 18.

**24** Kinyanjui (September 1984).

**25** See ERC Dissemination Unit (3 October 1984). This plan included a schedule of all activities, and assignment of specific staff responsibilities for the execution of the workshop.

**26** See ERC Dissemination Unit (November 1984).

**27** See ERC Dissemination Unit (December 1984, pp 5–6 and January 1985), p 1, for details concerning awards ceremonies and media coverage.

**28** ERC Dissemination Unit (January 1985), p 1.

**29** Clarkin (February 1985), p 30.

**30** ERC Dissemination Unit (December 1984 and January 1985).

**31** See Tapp (September 1984), pp 40–41.

**32** See Kinyanjui and Gamser, 'Trip Report: El Obeid – CARE Improved Stoves Program, 25–26 September 1984,' Khartoum: September 1984; and Kinyanjui and Gamser, 'The CARE El Obeid Stoves Project: Some Technical Observations,' Khartoum: September 1984.

**33** See *ibid*, and Kinyanjui (December 1984). The latter reference contains updated information on the programme from Kinyanjui's second visit to El Obeid that December.

**34** See Kinyanjui (December 1984); and Tapp (6 May 1985), pp 1–2.

**35** See Gaafar El Faki Ali and Matthew Gamser, 'Report: Field Trip to El Obeid, 11–12 December 1984,' Khartoum: 13 December 1984.

**36** CARE's follow-on grant proposal was contained in Tapp, 'Grant Proposal,' Khartoum: 6 May 1985. The ERC awarded CARE this grant on 27 June 1985.

**37** ACORD was awarded a grant of LS 1000 on 12 March 1985.

**38** A grant of LS 6198, awarded 14 April 1985.

**39** A grant of LS 55,055 awarded 18 May 1985.

**40** The FAO project involved was the 'Fuelwood Development for Energy in Sudan' project, sponsored by the government of the Netherlands and the FAO.

**41** Personal communication from the ERC Director, Dr El Tayeb Idris, 17 March

1986 – because of unsatisfactory progress, the CFA grant was terminated upon expenditure of the first tranche of funds (LS 20,000).
**42** See Kamal and Tyndal, pp 1–2.
**43** The depression in production in and around June 1985 is due to the Ramadan fasting period, during which time all production in Sudan is severely depressed.
**44** This is a best estimate. The NEA *National Energy Assessment* statistics indicate that there are 246,000 households in the Khartoum area. ERC staff personal experience has been that almost all Sudanese (as opposed to expatriate) homes in Khartoum have at least one charcoal stove, and that the average traditional stove lasts less than one year before it has to be replaced. The figure of 130,000 stoves is based upon the conservative estimate that half the households in Khartoum will purchase at least one new stove per year. No formal data about stove sales is available.
**45** Personal communication, Arthur Brown. Brown's consultancy report for SREP has yet to be published, largely because modifications suggested during his second visit to Sudan in January–February 1986 were not completed before the disruption of project activities by the American evacuation of assistance staff from the country.
**46** Georgia Institute of Technology, *Sudan Renewable Energy Project: Third Annual Report to USAID Khartoum* (Khartoum: GIT, November 1985), p 3. Its figures are based on the original University of Khartoum field test results, seen in Table 6.1.
**47** Since the author's departure from Sudan the ERC has carried out a major household stove user survey, in order to acquire more information from consumers. At the same time, it has continued its stove monitoring efforts, involving interviews with producers and distributers to keep informed as to the activities and opinions of these other technology users.

## Chapter 7

**1** Muna Ahmed Yassin, p 4. Yassin's report provides an excellent discussion of the ambiguities and internal inconsistencies contained in these laws, which have been a source of great difficulty for natural resource management in Sudan.
**2** Director of Forests, personal communication.
**3** *Ibid*. The Sudanese fiscal year was 1 July–30 June until the declaration of its transformation into an Islamic Republic in September 1983, at which time the nation moved partially to an islamic calendar year, and partially retained the old fiscal calendar. This caused great confusion in the national planning and finance sphere, which has not been completely resolved to this day. The ERC, for its own planning purposes, retained the July–June year.
**4** Those who participated in the meetings of this advisory group were: Dr M O El Sammani and Dr M Khoghali, Institute of Environmental Studies, University of Khartoum (sociologist and geographer, respectively); Mustafa Suleiman, Pastures and Range Management Department, Ministry of Agriculture; Dr Babiker A El Hassan, Forestry Department, University of Khartoum; Abdel Aziz Bayoumi, Desertification Control and Prevention Unit; Hamza Homoudi, National Energy Administration (later ERC Forestry Advisor); Dr Hassan Musnad, Dr Ahmed El Houri, and Dr Hamza El Amin, Forest Research Centre, Agricultural Research Corporation; Hannafi Obeid, Central Forestry Administration; Zein Ramadan, Central Forestry Administration; Kamal Osman Khalifa, Central Forestry Administration and Sudan Council of Churches (now Director of Forests, CFA); Haj Meki Awoda, Gum Arabic Corporation; and Gaafar El Faki Ali, National Energy Administration (later ERC, Assistant Coordinator of SREP and Head, Dissemination Unit).

**5** Formal articulation of the multi-faceted ERC programme was contained in Energy Research Council, Advisory Committee on Forestry/Fuelwood Production, 'Report to Technical Committee on Fuelwood/Forestry Programme Development,' Khartoum: 2 October 1983, which was reviewed and approved by the Technical Committee in its meeting of 16 November 1983. The ERC later refined its strategy in its 'Agroforestry Strategy' policy memorandum (Khartoum: February 1984).

**6** Abdel Aziz Bayoumi, 'The Role of Irrigated Agriculture Schemes in Combatting Desertification,' in Mary Clarkin (October 1985), p 29.

**7** Ali and Sid Ahmed, p 118; and Bayoumi.

**8** Ismail, pp 52–53.

**9** Ali and Sid Ahmed, p 118.

**10** Bayoumi, p 26.

**11** *Ibid*, p 25.

**12** *Ibid*, pp 23, 27.

**13** Foresters voiced this belief in their dominance of the discussions following the paper presentations in the AFTAH Conference (to be discussed later in this chapter), but the conference also provided a forum in which agriculturalists challenged the notion that they are inherently 'anti-tree'. See brief minutes of discussions found in Clarkin, ed., pp 91, 132–133. Discussion of the progress of the Seleit scheme grant project later in the chapter also belies the foresters' notion that agriculturalists obstructed afforestation measures.

**14** See Homoudi and Gamser (18–21 November 1984). Assistance to regional forestry efforts from the Sudan Council of Churches in 1981–1985 helped these projects to progress while much Gezira province work was in decline. However, the completion of the SCC aid programme left the regional authorities with insufficient materials and funds to sustain the projects. Recent ERC grant support to the region may help to prevent further degradation, and encourage new afforestation efforts.

**15** The Seleit Scheme was awarded LS 42,365 on 15 November 1983. A follow-on grant of LS 25,050 was awarded on 22 January 1985. It is the author's understanding that a further grant of LS 20,000 was awarded in April of 1986. The declining amounts of the grants reflect the Seleit Scheme's growing assumption of financial responsibility for the successful forestry efforts.

**16** Hamza Homoudi, personal correspondence, 26 March 1986.

**17** It is difficult and potentially misleading to make direct comparisons between the work at Seleit and forestry in schemes such as Gezira, because different environmental conditions, cropping patterns and the varying scales of these operations create somewhat different work contexts. Moreover, the Gezira scheme is made up of a large number of smallholder plots controlled by a central board, while the Seleit scheme has no tenant farmers, consisting entirely of centrally-controlled mechanized cereal and vegetable cropping. In addition, the two-year old Seleit forestry project has another four years before its first harvest of its woodlots, as well as a planting programme that may or may not proceed according to the pattern of the past two years, which make its total benefits to the overall scheme uncertain. Nonetheless, the progress of forestry work on the Seleit Scheme has greatly impressed both foresters and agriculturalists in Sudan.

**18** 'Standing timber' refers to growing stock (trees) sold while still in the ground. In such purchases the buyer is obliged to carry out all harvesting operations, and to bear all the expenses of such. The Guneid sale prices were provided for the author in a personal communication from Hamza Homoudi, 26 March 1986.

**19** Seleit's initial enthusiasm for the project has been described in an earlier section. In 1985 the corporation changed directors, which could have altered its support for the project. However, the new director, after viewing the work to date, became as supportive as his predecessor. His report on the project belies Bayoumi's pessimistic description of agriculturalist's attitude to forestry:

the demands of the human population on forests, rivers, agricultural land and so forth are increasing while the supplies from the natural resources are often used unwisely. For example: trees which control soil erosion and help land to retain moisture and fertility are cut down excessively. Therefore, the demand for this resource should be met by planting trees. So, like other countries around the world Sudan is now trying to solve these problems and take steps to stop the incorrect use of its natural resources. One of these steps is the incorporation of tree planting in big agricultural projects. One of these big agricultural projects is the Seleit Scheme. (Mustafa Bedawi Bashir, 'A Note on Seleit's Reforestation and Shelterbelt Programmes,' in Clarkin, ed., p 80).

It is doubtful that Bayoumi could have written a more impassioned plea for the cause of forestry himself, but these words come from an agriculturalist.

**20** A more detailed description of the project can be found in Tapp (1984), p 24.

**21** *Ibid*, p 24. Note that Tapp points out that the UN project did not establish a sound monitoring apparatus to confirm whether its seedlings distributed to farmers survived or perished. This point is important in light of the observations of the project's problems to follow in the text.

**22** See Bradford *et al*.

**23** See *ibid*.

**24** See *ibid*.

**25** This point is also made in Tapp (1984), pp 25–27.

**26** El Sammani *et al*, pp 43–44.

**27** An additional confusion was presented by the 'proposal' developed by the El Sammani team, which had visited the area and recommended that the ERC consider initiating a project in Um Inderaba. This 'proposal' (which, in the ERC's sense, it was not, as it did not come from the village itself), contained a basic description of a million dollar project for the village, including new buildings, several vehicles, and irrigation works. The team had talked to the villagers about these development ideas, so the ERC team's subsequent discussion of a far smaller, village-devised and implemented effort, contradicted the earlier message. The proposal is contained in *ibid*, pp 39–68. The confusion and ire that resulted from the ERC's different, grant-based conception of village forestry, is chronicled in Bradford *et al*.

**28** See Bradford *et al*.

**29** An ERC grant of LS 10,500 was awarded Um Inderaba on 18 March 1984.

**30** See Homoudi and Gamser (February 1985).

**31** The technical potential of *Acacia senegal* for multi-product exploitation is well described in National Academy of Sciences (1980), pp 102–103.

**32** See Bradford, pp 7–9.

**33** Adams (31 March 1985).

**34** See El Tahir.

**35** Georgia Institute of Technology, *Sudan Renewable Energy Project: Third Annual Report*, p 5.

**36** See Hassan and Gamser.

**37** Gamser (August 1984).

**38** See Adams (September 1985).

**39** Gamser, 'Notes from 21 August 1984 Discussion'.

**40** See Adams (September 1985).

**41** ERC Advisory Committee on Forestry/Fuelwood Production, 'Report to Technical Committee'.

**42** Moghran nursery was awarded a grant of LS 64,450 on 15 January 1984 (the largest single REDG grant); and Soba nursery was awarded a grant of LS 45,940 on 4 April 1984.

**43** Personal communication, Hamza Homoudi, Khalafalla Sid Ahmed and Jim Adams (ERC foresters).

**44** Personal communication, Brad Tyndal and Mary Clarkin of the Dissemination Unit, July 1985, and subsequent personal communication from Jim Adams, 6 March 1986.

**45** Bayoumi, Khalifa and Saleem; El Hassan, El Sammani, and Suliman; ERC Dissemination Unit (June 1984).

**46** Sid Ahmed; and Ali and Sid Ahmed, pp 115–131.

**47** Earl (1985).

**48** See, for example, Mahmoud, p 29; and Tyndal (July 1985), p 42.

**49** Tyndal (March 1985), p 3.

**50** *Ibid*, pp 8–9.

**51** Energy Research Council (February 1985).

**52** The Blue Nile farmer, El Daw Idris, received a grant of LS 750 on 1 May 1985; and Markha Awaj Ed Dareb village received a grant of LS 15,000 on 21 August 1985. The PLAN proposal was considered after the author's departure from Sudan.

**53** ERC, *Basic Tree Nursery Techniques*, p 6.

**54** Clarkin (October 1985), p iii.

**55** See Homoudi and Gamser (June 1985).

**56** See El Lakani, pp 43–48.

**57** See AFTAH discussion notes in Clarkin, ed, pp 132–133.

**58** El Tayeb Idris, pp 136–137.

**59** Georgia Institute of Technology, *Monthly Reports: SREP*, September and November 1985; January 1986.

**60** Homoudi, personal correspondence, 26 March 1986.

**61** Ali and Sid Ahmed, pp 120–121, 128. The author has adjusted their figures to remove Northern Region contributions. However, the demand figures, based on National Energy Administration household survey extrapolations, may be high (see discussion of the problems of these figures at the end of Chapter 6), so the potential contribution could be much greater than even Ali and Sid Ahmed suggest.

**62** For information on the actual increases in crop performance obtained in Egyptian shelterbelt trials, see El Lakani, p 47; and Heikal *et al*.

## Chapter 8

**1** Kanter, pp 34–35.

**2** Peters and Waterman, p 12.

**3** Richards, *Indigenous Agricultural Revolution*, p 12.

**4** FAO, *Tree Growing by Rural People*, p 2.

**5** *Ibid*, p 31.

**6** The problem of academic 'professionalism' in itself constituting a negative influence on technology development, through erecting barriers to R & D-user interaction, is discussed in a thought-provoking work by Robert Chambers (December 1985).

**7** Kanter, p 64.

# Bibliography

Abd El Nour, Hassan Osman, and Satti, Kamal Mohamed Osman. *Charcoal Production in Blue Nile Province*. Khartoum: Energy Research Council, November 1984.

Abd El Nour, Hassan Osman. 'Report on Current Charcoal Production Components in the Blue Nile.' In Earl, D E, *Report on Charcoal Production*, Appendix V, pp 37–57.

Adams, Jim. 'Report on Small Farm Grants.' Khartoum: September 1985.

Adams, Jim. 'Um Tureibat Monthly Renewable Energy Report.' Khartoum: 31 March 1985.

Agarwal, Bina. *Cold Hearths and Barren Slopes: The Woodfuel Crisis in the Third World*. New Delhi: Allied Publishers Private Ltd, 1986.

Agarwal, Bina. 'Diffusion of Rural Innovations; Some Analytical Issues and the Case of Wood Burning Stoves.' *World Development* 11:4 (1983): 359–376.

Agarwal, Bina. 'The Woodfuel Problem and the Diffusion of Rural Innovations.' Final Report submitted to the UK Tropical Products Institute. Mimeo, Science Policy Research Unit, Falmer, UK, November 1980.

Alassam, M. 'Decentralization for Development: The Sudanese Experience.' Paper presented at the United Nations Interregional Seminar on Decentralization for Development. Khartoum: Democratic Republic of Sudan, 14–18 September 1981.

Ali, Amal Tijani. 'A Study of the Organization of the Energy Sector.' Mimeo, National Energy Administration, Khartoum, September 1984.

Ali, Gaafar El Faki, and Huff, Claudia. *Canun el Duga: Improved Charcoal Stoves for the Sudan*. Khartoum: Energy Research Council, December 1984.

Ali, Gaafar El Faki. *Charcoal Marketing and Production in Blue Nile Province*. Khartoum: Energy Research Council, August 1985.

Ali, Gaafar El Faki, and Gamser, Matthew. Memorandum to Dissemination Unit, re: Charcoal Stove Dissemination Team. Khartoum: 11 April 1984.

Ali, Gaafar El Faki, and Gamser, Matthew. Memorandum to ERC Forestry and Dissemination Staff. Subject: Khartoum Area Small Farmer Forestry Discussion. Khartoum: 31 January 1985.

Ali, Gaafar El Faki, and Sid Ahmed, Khalafalla. 'Potential for Agriculture and Forestry Integration in Irrigated Schemes of Northern Sudan.' In Clarkin, ed, pp 115–131.

Ali, Gaafar El Faki, and Gamser, Matthew. 'Report: Field Trip to El Obeid, 11–12 December 1984.' Khartoum: 13 December 1984.

Allen, Thomas J. *Managing the Flow of Technology: Technology Transfer and the Dissemination of Technological Information Within the Research and Development Organization.* Cambridge, MA: The MIT Press, 1977.

Allen, Thomas J. 'Performance of Information Channels in the Transfer of Technology.' *Industry Management Review* 8:1 (Fall 1966): 87–98.

Ashby, Jacqueline A. 'Participation of Small Farmers in Technology Assessment.' Report on a Special Project of the International Fertilizer Development Center, in Collaboration with the International Center for Tropical Agriculture and the Instituto Colombiano Agropecuario. Mimeo, CIAT, 1984.

Bandyopedhyay, J., and Shiva, Vandana. 'Growing Wisely or Growing Well? The Case Against Eucalyptus.' *Indian Express*, 15 July 1984, Express Magazine pp 1, 6.

Bannerman, Robert H. 'The Role of Traditional Medicine in Primary Health Care.' In Bannerman *et al*, pp 318–327.

Bannerman, Robert; Burton, John; and Wen-Chieh, Ch'en, eds. *Traditional Medicine and Health Care Coverage: A Reader for Health Administrators and Practitioners.* Geneva: World Health Organization, 1983.

Barnett, Andrew. 'The Choice of Energy Conversion Technologies for Small-Scale Pumping Systems – A Review.' Mimeo, Science Policy Research Unit, Falmer, UK, December 1985.

Barnett, Andrew; Bell, Martin, and Hoffman, Kurt. *Rural Energy and the Third World: A Review of Social Science Research and Technology Policy Problems.* Oxford: Pergamon Press, 1982.

Bashir, Mustafa Bedawi. 'A Note on Seleit's Reforestation and Shelterbelt Programmes.' In Clarkin, ed, pp 79–84.

Bayoumi, Abdel Aziz. 'The Role of Irrigated Agriculture Schemes in combatting Desertification.' In Clarkin, ed, pp 15–40.

Bayoumi, Abdel Aziz; Khalifa, Kamal Osman; and Saleem, Ali Ahmed. *Study for the Establishment of Forestry Plantations, Shelterbelts, and Canal Plantations in the Northern Region.* Khartoum: Energy Research Council, February 1984.

Bell, Martin. 'The Exploitation of Indigenous Knowledge, or the Indigenous Exploitation of Knowledge: Whose Use of What for What?' *IDS Bulletin* 10:2 (January 1979): 44–50.

Bell, R M [Martin]. *Science, Technology and Future Development in the Third World: Key Issues for Policy, Institutional Development, and Management.* SPRU Study Material on Science and Technology Policy and Policy Research in Third World Countries: Introductory Module (Review Paper). Falmer: Science Policy Research Unit, University of Sussex, October 1985.

Belshaw, Deryke. 'Talking Indigenous Technology Seriously: The Case of Inter-Cropping Techniques in East Africa.' *IDS Bulletin* 10:2 (January 1979): 24–27.

Bhatia, Ramesh, and Pereira, Armand. *Socio-Economic Aspects of Renewable Energy Technologies* (final draft). ILO World Employment Programme, Technology and Employment Branch. Geneva: ILO, November 1985.

146

Biggs, Stephen. 'Informal R and D.' *Ceres* 13:4 (July–August 1980): 23–26.

Black, Ronald P. 'The IRRI Agricultural Equipment Program.' Mimeo, Denver Research Institute, Denver, CO, 2 November 1976.

Bonnet, Didier C. L. 'Nature of the R & D/Marketing Co-Operation in the Design of Technologically Advanced New Industrial Products.' *R & D Management* 16:2 (April 1986): 117–126.

Bradford, Lester Ezra. *SREP: Report on Fuelwood Production, December 1983–September 1984.* Khartoum: Energy Research Council, September 1984.

Bradford, Lester; Homoudi, Hamza; El Gizouli, Mohammed Hassan; and Gamser, Matthew. 'Trip Report: Northern Kordofan Forestry Study, 6–13 February 1984.' Khartoum: February 1984.

Brammer, Hugh. 'Some Innovations Don't Wait for Experts.' *Ceres* 13:2 (March–April 1980): 24–28.

Brokensha, David W; Warren, D W; and Werner, Oscar, eds. *Indigenous Knowledge Systems and Development.* Lanham, MD: University Press of America, Inc, 1980.

Bromley, Ray. 'Introduction – The Urban Informal Sector: Why Is It Worth Discussing?' *World Development* 6:9/10 (September–October 1978): 1033–1040.

Brown, Lester R, and Wolf, Edward C. *Reversing Africa's Decline.* Worldwatch Paper No 65. Washington, DC: Worldwatch Institute, June 1985.

Catterson, T M; Gulick, F A; and Resch, T. 'Desertification – Rethinking Forestry Strategy in Africa: Experience Drawn from USAID Activities.' Paper prepared for FAO Expert Consultation on the Role of Forestry in Combatting Desertification, Saltillo, Mexico, 24–28 June 1985.

Chambers, Robert, and Jiggens, Janice. 'Agriculture Research for Resource-Poor Farmers: A Parsimonious Paradigm.' IDS, Paper for Discussion, 27 November 1985.

Chambers, Robert. 'Normal Professionalism, New Paradigms, and Development.' IDS, Paper for the Seminar on Poverty, Development, and Food: Towards the 21st Century, in Honour of the 75th Birthday of Professor H W Singer, 13–14 December 1985.

Chaudhuri, Shekhar. 'Technological Innovation in a Research Laboratory in India: A Case Study.' *Research Policy* 15:2 (April 1986): 89–103.

Clark, Kim B. The Interaction of Design Hierarchies and Market Concepts in Technological Evolution.' *Research Policy* 14:5 (October 1985): 235–251.

Clark, Norman. *The Political Economy of Science and Technology.* Oxford: Basil Blackwell, 1985.

Clarke, Robin, ed *Wood Stove Dissemination: Proceedings of the Conference Held at Wolfheze, the Netherlands.* London: IT Publications, 1985.

Clarkin, Mary, ed *Proceedings of AFTAH: Agriculture and Forestry, Towards an Abundant Harvest. A Seminar on the Integration of Agriculture and Forestry in the Irrigated Sector of the Sudan, 10–13 August 1985, Grand Hotel, Khartoum, Sudan.* Khartoum: Energy Research Council, October 1985.

Clarkin, Mary. 'Stove Workshop: Improving Standards.' *Sudanow* (February 1985): 30.

Cohen, John M, and Uphoff, Norman T. 'Participation's Place in Rural Development: Seeking Clarity Through Specificity.' *World Development* 8:3 (March 1980): 213–236.

Conahan, Frank C. (Director, US General Accounting Office). Letter to M Peter McPherson, Administrator, Agency for International Development (Ref: B–208537). Subject: AID's renewable Energy Projects (GAO/ID–82–57). 13 August 1982 (mimeo).

Deudney, Daniel, and Flavin, Christopher. *Renewable Energy: The Power to Choose*. New York: W W Norton & Company, 1983.

DEVRES. *The Socio-Economic Context of Fuelwood Use in Small Rural Communities*. AID Evaluation Special Study No. 1. Washington, DC: US Agency for International Development, August 1980.

Diop, Lamine. Improved Stoves in Senegal.' In Clarke, Robin, ed, pp 175–181.

Douglas, J, Sholto, and Hart, Robert A de J *Forest Farming: Towards a Solution to Problems of World Hunger and Conservation*. London: Intermediate Technology Publications, 1984.

Earl, D E *Forest Energy and Economic Development*. Oxford: Clarendon Press, 1975.

Earl, D E *Report on Charcoal Production*. Khartoum: Energy Research Council, February 1984.

Earl, Derek E. *Sudan – The Economics of Wood Energy Production on Mechanized Farms*. Khartoum: Energy Research Council, April 1985.

Eckholm, Erik P. *Losing Ground: Environmental Stress and World Food Prospects*. New York: W W Norton & Company, 1976.

The *Economist* Intelligence Unit. *Quarterly Economic Review of Sudan: Annual Supplement 1985*. London: The Economist Publications Ltd, 1985.

Eisa, El Tayeb Idris. 'How the SREP Grants Program Works in Agroforestry Projects.' In Clarkin, ed, pp 135–138.

El Hassan, B A; El Sammani, M O; and Suliman, M. *Village Biomass Needs: Northern Kordofan Region*. Khartoum: Energy Research Council, July 1984.

El Lakani, M Hosni. 'Agriculture and Forestry: the Egyptian Experience.' In Clarkin, ed, pp 43–48.

El Sammani, M O; El Hassan, B A; and Suliman, M. 'Village Forestry Project (Integrated Village Development)'. Study and proposal submitted to Advisory Committee on Forestry/Fuelwood Production. Khartoum: September, 1983.

El Tahir, Issam Haj. 'Trip Report: Nahud, Turba Hamra, El Khoue [sic], 31 August – 2 September 1985.' Khartoum: CARE Sudan, September 1985.

Energy Research Council. Agroforestry Strategy. Khartoum: February 1984.

Energy Research Council. *Basic Tree Nursery Techniques* (English and Arabic, 2 versions). Khartoum: Energy Research Council, February 1985.

148

Energy Research Council. 'Description of Grants Program Under Sudan Renewable Energy Project.' Khartoum: 9 December 1983.

Energy Research Council. 'Internal Review of Grant Proposals Under Sudan Renewable Energy Project.' Khartoum: 9 December 1983.

Energy Research Council, Advisory Committee on Forestry/Fuelwood Production. 'Report to Technical Committee on Fuelwood/Forestry Programme Development.' Khartoum: Passed by Advisory Committee 2 October 1983, reviewed and passed by Technical Committee, 16 November 1983.

Energy Research Council, Dissemination Unit. 'Final Report: Khartoum Stovemakers Training Workship for *Canun El Duga*, November 3–15 1984.' Khartoum: Energy Research Council, December 1984.

Energy Research Council, Dissemination Unit. 'How to Establish Shelterbelts' (Arabic). Pamphlet, Khartoum: June 1984.

Energy Research Council, Dissemination Unit. 'How to Plant Trees' (Arabic). Pamphlet, Khartoum: June 1984.

Energy Research Council, Dissemination Unit. 'Implementation Plan for Khartoum Stovemakers Training Workshop.' 3 October 1984.

Energy Research Council, Dissemination Unit. 'Khartoum-Area Stovemakers Workshops for *Canun El Duga*.' January 1985.

Energy Research Council, Dissemination Unit (Ali, Gaafar El Faki; Suliman, Soumaya; Mahmoud, Awatif; Majoub, Fadia; El-Beshir, El-Tayeb; Huff, Claudia; and Gamser, Matthew). *Trainer's Manual for Canun El Duga*. Khartoum: Energy Research Council, November 1984.

Energy Research Council, Dissemination Unit. *Trainees' Manual for Canun El Duga (Arabic)*. Khartoum: Energy Research Council, November 1984; revised edition July 1985.

Energy Research Council, Technical Committee. Minutes of Meetings, 14 March 1984, and 17 July 1984.

FAO. *Forestry and Rural Development*. Forestry Paper No. 26. Rome: FAO, 1981.

FAO. *Forestry for Local Community Development*. Forestry Paper No. 7. Rome: FAO, 1978.

FAO. *Forestry for Rural Communities*. Rome: FAO, 1978.

FAO. 'Policy, Institutions, and Socio-Economic Considerations: An Overview.' Background Paper No. 6 for Expert Consultation on the Role of Forestry in Combatting Desertification, Saltillo, Mexico, 24–28 June 1985. Rome: FAO, 1985.

FAO. *Simple Technologies for Charcoal Making*. Forestry Paper No. 41. Rome: FAO, 1983.

FAO. 'Summary Report of the Expert Consultation on the Role of Forestry in Combatting Desertification.' Saltillo, Mexico: FAO, 24–28 June 1985.

FAO. *Tree Growing by Rural People*. Forestry Paper No. 64. Rome: FAO, 1985.

Folch-Lyon, Evelyn; de la Macorra, Luis; and Shearer, S. Bruce. 'Focus

Group and Survey Research on Family Planning in Mexico.' *Studies in Family Planning* 12:12 (December 1981): 409–432.

Foley, Gerald. *Charcoal Making in Developing Countries*. Earthscan Energy Information Programme, Technical Report No. 5. London: IIED, 1986.

Foley, Gerald, and Moss, Patricia. *Improved Cooking Stoves in Developing Countries*. Earthscan Energy Information Programme, Technical Report No. 2. London: IIED, 1983.

Fransman, Martin, and King, Kenneth, eds *Technological Capability in the Third World*. London: The MacMillan Press Ltd, 1984.

Fransman, Martin. 'Technological Capability in the Third World: An Overview and Introduction to Some of the Issues Raised in This Book.' In Fransman and King, eds, pp 3–30.

Freeman, Christopher. *The Economics of Industrial Innovation* (2nd edition). London: Frances Pinter (Publishers) Limited, 1982.

French, David. 'Context Monitoring: The Energy Studies Unit and the Malawi Wood Energy Project.' Mimeo, Energy Studies Unit, Lilongwe, Malawi, August 1984.

Friedmann, John. 'Planning as Social Learning.' In Korten and Klaus, eds, pp 189–194.

Gamser, Matthew. Journal, Sudan. 5 volumes, November 1982–October 1985.

Gamser, Matthew. Memorandum to Dr. Yahia Hamid: Minutes of 29 February 1984 Meeting. Khartoum: 1 March 1984.

Gamser, Matthew. Memorandum to Files, re: visit of manufacturer/ artisans interested in charcoal stoves contest. Khartoum: 30 January 1984.

Gamser, Matthew. Notes from 21 August 1984 Discussion of ERC Forestry/Fuelwood Activities (present: ERC Director, ERC Assistant Director, ERC Forestry Advisor, Dissemination Unit Head, Lester Bradford, and author). Khartoum: August 1984.

Georgia Institute of Technology. Monthly Reports, Sudan Renewable Energy Project. Khartoum: GIT, November 1982 – January 1986.

Georgia Institute of Technology, Engineering Experiment Station [now Georgia Tech Research Institute]. *Proposal for Sudan Rural Renewable Energy Project. Part 1: Technical Proposal*. Atlanta, GA: Georgia Institute of Technology, February 1982.

Georgia Institute of Technology. 'Monthly Reports: SREP'. Khartoum: GIT, September 1985, November 1985, January 1986.

Georgia Institute of Technology. *Sudan Renewable Energy Project: Third Annual Report to USAID Khartoum*. Khartoum: GIT, November 1985.

Gross, William. 'Memo to Files, re Contact Report: Visit at National Council for Research.' Khartoum: National Energy Administration, 10 November 1981.

Gross, William. 'Memo to Mohamed El Amin Mukhtar, re The Rural Renewable Energy Project and the Institute of Energy Research.' Khartoum: National Energy Administration, 17 November 1981.

Gurdon, Charles. *Sudan in Transition: A Political Risk Analysis.* The Economist Intelligence Unit, Political Risk Series, Report No. 226. London: The Economist Publications Ltd, 1986.

Gardiner, Paul, and Rothwell, Roy. 'Tough Customers: Good Designs.' *Design Studies* 6:1 (January 1985): 7–17.

Hall, Mike, and Percy, Steve. 'Policy Up a Gum Tree.' *The Guardian,* Third World Review, 19 April 1986.

Harden, Blaine. 'Sudan's Economic Condition Worsens.' *The Washington Post:* 6 May 1986.

Harris, John R, and Rowe, M P. 'Entrepreneurial Patterns in the Nigerian Sawmilling Industry.' In Teriba and Kayode, eds, pp 177–197.

Harris, John R. 'Nigerian Enterprise in the Printing Industry.' In Teriba and Kayode, eds, pp 198–210.

Hart, Keith. 'Informal Income Opportunities and Urban Employment in Ghana.' *The Journal of Modern African Studies* 11:1 (March 1973): 61–90.

Harwood, Richard R. *Small Farm Development: Understanding and Improving Farming Systems in the Humid Tropics.* IADS Development Oriented Literature Series. Boulder, CO: Westview Press, 1979.

Hassan, Hassan Wardi, and Peterson, Donald B. Memorandum to ERC/ SREP Project Leaders. Subject: Work Plans. Khartoum: 28 January 1984.

Hassan, Hassan Wardi, and Gamser, Matthew. Memorandum to Technical Committee. Subject. Small Farmer Grant Proposals. Khartoum: 18 January 1984.

Hassan, Hassan Wardi. Summary, SREP Review Meeting, 7 December 1983. Khatoum: December 1983.

Heikal, Ibrahim A; Imam, Mohamed El Said; El Sherbini, Gamal El Din H.; Shahata, Mohamed S; and Soliman, Galal M. 'The Influence of Shelterbelts on the Yield of Barley in Tahreer Province.' Mimeo. Cairo: Agricultural Research Centre, 1982.

Herrera, Amilcar O. 'The Generation of Technologies in Rural Areas.' *World Development* 9:1 (January 1981): 21–36.

Hinman, George; Icerman, Larry; and Seig, Louis. 'Commercializing New Technology-Based Start-Up Industries.' *Research Management* 29:1 (January–February 1986): 31–35.

Holt, Knut. 'User-Oriented Product Innovation – Some Research Findings.' *Technovation* 3:3 (August 1985): 199–208.

Homoudi, Hamza, and Gamser, Matthew. Trip Report: Egypt Agroforestry Study Tour, 30 April – 13 May 1985. Khartoum: June 1985.

Homoudi, Hamza, and Gamser, Matthew. Trip Report: Forestry/Fuelwood Visit to Northern Regional and Local Government, 18–21 November 1984. Khartoum: November 1984.

Homoudi, Hamza, and Gamser, Matthew. Trip Report: Um Inderaba Visit, 24 February 1985. Khartoum: February 1985.

Hoskins, Marilyn. 'Social Forestry in West Africa: Myths and Realities.'

Paper presented at the annual meeting of the American Association for the Advancement of Science, Washington, DC, 8 January 1982.

Howes, Michael, and Chambers, Robert. 'Indigenous Technical Knowledge: Analysis, Implications and Issues.' *IDS Bulletin* 10:2 (January 1979): 5–11.

Howes, Michael. *Rural Energy Surveys in the Third World: A Critical Review of Issues and Methods*. International Development Research Centre, Manuscript Report. Ottawa: IDRC, May 1985.

Howes, Michael. 'The Uses of Indigenous Technology in Development.' *IDS Bulletin* 10:2 (January 1979): 12–23.

Huff, Claudia H. *Dissemination Consultancy Report – SREP: 12 September – 12 December 1984*. Khartoum: Energy Research Council, December 1984.

Hyman, Eric L. 'The Strategy of Decentralized Production and Distribution of Improved Charcoal Stoves in Kenya.' *World Development*, forthcoming.

Imam, Mohamed El Said, and Azzouz, Sayed. 'Windbreaks and Shelterbelts: Their Effects in a Useful Way on the Agricultural Crops and Soil Conservation.' Unpublished report. Cairo: Agricultural Research Centre, Timber Trees Research Section, Horticultural Research Institute, 1981.

Ismail, Badr El Din. 'Rahad Agricultural Corporation's Experience with the Integration of Agriculture and Forestry.' In Clarkin, ed, pp 51–55.

Jantsch, Erich. *The Self-Organizing Universe: Scientific and Human Implications of the Emerging Paradigm of Evolution*. Oxford: Pergamon Press, 1980.

Joseph, Steven, and Hassrick, Philip. *Burning Issues: Implementing Pilot Stove Programmes. A Guide for Eastern Africa*. London: UNICEF/IT Publications, 1984.

Joseph, S D; Shanahan, Y M; and Stewart, W. *The Stove Project Manual: Planning and Implementation*. London: Intermediate Technology Publications, 1985.

Kamal, Amin, and Tyndal, Brad. Shendi Trip, July 1985: Update on the Stove Programme. Khartoum: July 1985.

Kanter, Rosabeth Moss. *The Change Masters: Corporate Entrepreneurs at Work*. London: Unwin Paperbacks, 1985.

Khosla, Ashok. 'A Delivery System for Appropriate Technologies.' In Clarke, Robin, ed, pp 90–98.

King, Kenneth. *The African Artisan: A Study of Training, Technology and the Informal Sector in Kenya*. Edinburgh: University of Edinburgh, Centre of African Studies, 1975. Later published by Heinemann, London, 1977.

Kinyanjui, Maxwell, and Gamser, Matthew. The CARE El Obeid Stoves Project: Some Technical Observations. Khartoum: September 1984.

Kinyanjui, Maxwell. *Consultant's Report on SREP Charcoal Stoves*. Kenya: Energy/Development International, May 1984.

Kinyangui, Maxwell. 'The 'Jiko' Industry in Kenya.' In Clarke, Robin, ed, pp 150–157.

Kinyanjui, Maxwell. Proposed Program for Khartoum Stovemakers Training Workshop. Khartoum: September 1984.

Kinyanjui, Maxwell. Report on Advisory Visit to the CARE-Sudan/SREP Project, El Obeid. Khartoum: December 1984.

Kinyanjui, Maxwell, and Gamser, Matthew. Trip Report: El Obeid – CARE Improved Stoves Project, 25–26 September 1984. Khartoum: September 1984.

Ki-Zerbo, Jacqueline. 'Improved Cooking Stoves in the Sahel.' In Clarke, Robin, ed, pp 105–111.

Kline, Stephen J. 'Innovation Is Not a Linear Process.' *Research Management* 28:4 (July–August 1985): 36–45.

Korten, David C, and Klauss, Rudi, eds *People Centered Development: Contributions Toward Theory and Planning Frameworks*. Connecticut: Kumarian Press, 1984.

Korten, David C, and Carner, George. 'Planning Frameworks for People-Centred Development.' In Korten and Klaus, eds, pp 201–209.

Korten, David C. 'Rural Development Programming: The Learning Process Approach.' In Korten and Klaus, eds, pp 176–188.

Langrish, J; Gibbons, M; Evans, W G; and Jevons, F R. *Wealth from Knowledge: Studies of Innovation in Industry*. London: The MacMillan press, Ltd, 1972.

Lehman, James, and Aclimandos, Anis. *Present and Future Manpower Needs of the Renewable Energy Institute of the Energy Research Council – A Preliminary Assessment*. Khartoum: Sudan Renewable Energy Project, 2–16 August 1983.

Li, Yao Tsu, and Blais, Roger. 'The Innovation Galore, from Classroom to the Shop Floor.' *Technovation* 1:4 (August 1982): 255–273.

Lillywhite, Malcolm, and Lillywhite, Linda. 'Consultant Report: Rural Renewable Energy Project.' Khartoum: US Agency for International Development, 1980.

Lindberg, Chris, and Hobgood, Thomas. 'Forestry Sector Development Issues in the Gambia.' Paper prepared for USAID Workshop on Forestry Program Evaluation, Lome, Togo, 7–11 May 1984. Mimeo, Lome, Togo, May 1984.

Lowdermilk, Max K. *Improved Irrigation Management: Why Involve Farmers?* ODI Irrigation Management Network Paper No. 11c. London: ODI, May 1985.

MacKerron, Gordon, and Thomas, Steve. 'Why Is the Economic Experience of Nuclear Power So Variable?' Mimeo, Energy Policy Programme, Science Policy Research Unit, Falmer, January 1986.

Mahiti Team. 'A Question: Why Is Social Forestry Not Social?' Paper prepared for the Ford Foundation Workshop on Social Forestry and Voluntary Agencies, 13–15 April 1983, Badkal Lake, Haryana. Ahmedabad: Mahiti Project, 1983.

Mahler, Halfden (Director-General, World Health Organization). 'Forward'. In Bannerman *et al*, pp 7–8.

Mahmoud, Awatif. 'Training Very Useful.' *Sudanow* (April 1985): 29.

Majoub, Fadia. 'Laboratory Tests of Improved Stove Designs.' Mimeo, ERC, Khartoum, September, 1983.

Makuria, Getachew. 'Wood-Stove Dissemination: The Ethiopian Experience.' In Clarke, Robin, ed, pp 167–174.

Marris, Peter, and Somerset, Anthony. *African Businessmen: A Study of Entrepreneurship and Development in Kenya.* London: Routledge & Keegan Paul, 1971.

Marx, Karl, and Engels, Friedrich. *The Communist Manifesto.* Samuel Moore translation, introduction by A J P Taylor. London: Penguin Books, 1967.

Massé, Rene. 'The Dissemination of Improved Wood Stoves.' In Clarke, Robin, ed, pp 21–28.

Matlon, Peter; Cantrell, Ronald; King, David; and Benoit-Catlin, Michel, eds. *Coming Full Circle: Farmers' Participation in the Development of a Technology.* Ottawa: IDRC, 1984.

Mead, Donald C. 'Of Contracts and Subcontracts: Small Firms in Vertically Dis-Integrated Production/Distribution Systems in LDC's.' *World Development* 12:11/12 (November–December 1984): 1095–1106.

Mowery, David, and Rosenberg, Nathan. 'The Influence of Market Demand Upon Innovation: A Critical Review of Some Empirical Studies.' In Rosenberg, Nathan, *Inside the Black Box*, pp 193–241.

Nasr El Din, Shadia, and Clarkin, Mary. Canun El Duga Status Reports. Khartoum: March – September 1985.

Nasr El Din, Shadia. *A Report on the Improved Charcoal Stove Project.* Khartoum: Energy Research Council, December 1983.

National Academy of Sciences. *Energy for Rural Development: Renewable Resources and Alternative Technologies for Developing Countries.* Washington, DC: National Academy Press, 1976.

National Academy of Sciences. *Environmental Change in the West African Sahel.* Washington, DC: National Academy Press, 1983.

National Academy of Sciences. *Firewood Crops: Shrub and Tree Species for Energy Production.* Washington, DC: National Academy Press, 1980.

National Academy of Sciences. *Supplement: Energy for Rural Development – Renewable and Alternative Technologies for Developing Countries.* Washington, DC: National Academy Press, 1981.

National Energy Administration/Ministry of Energy and Mining. *Sudan National Energy Assessment. Annex 1: Base Year (1980) Supply/Demand Balances and Demand Projection Methodology.* Khartoum: NEA/MEM, March 1983.

Navaratna, Harishini. 'The Sarvodaya Stove Project in Sri Lanka.' In Clarke, Robin, ed, pp 139–149.

Nelson, Harold D, ed. *Sudan: A Country Study.* The American University Foreign Area Studies. Third Edition. Washington, DC: US Government Printer, 1982.

Nelson, Richard R, and Winter, Sidney C. *An Evolutionary Theory of Economic Change*. Cambridge, MA: Harvard University Press, 1982.

Odufalu, J O. 'Indigenous Enterprise in Nigerian Manufacturing.' *The Journal of Modern African Studies* 9:4 (December 1971): 593–607.

O'Keefe, Liz, and Howes, Michael. 'A Select Annotated Bibliography: Indigenous Technical Knowledge in Development.' *IDS Bulletin* 10:2 (January 1979): 51–58.

Page, John M, Jr. 'Economies of Scale, Income Distribution, and Small-Enterprise Promotion in Ghana's Timber Industry.' *Food Research Institute Studies* 16:3 (1977–1978): 159–182.

Pereira, Armand. 'Organisational and Institutional Aspects of Improved Stoves.' In Bhatia and Pereira, Chapter 8.

Peters, Thomas J, and Waterman, Robert H, Jr. *In Search of Excellence: Lessons from America's Best-Run Companies*. New York: Warner Books, Inc., 1984.

Peterson, Donald B. 'Background Paper: Sudan Renewable Energy Project.' Information paper for USAID Khartoum Director. Khartoum: 29 November 1983.

Powell, John W. 'Wood Waste as an Energy Source for Ghana.' In Brown, Norman L., ed, *Renewable Energy Resources and Rural Applications in the Developing World*. Boulder, CO: Westview Press, 1978, pp 115–128.

Prasad, K Krishna. 'Stove Design for Improved Dissemination.' In Clarke, ed, pp 59–74.

Pryor, C A. [USAID East Africa Regional Energy Advisor]. Memorandum to Jay Carter [USAID Energy Advisor, Khartoum], Donald Peterson, and Matthew Gamser. Subject: SREP Implementation. Khartoum: 15 November 1983.

Quinn, James Brian. 'Managing Innovation: Controlled Chaos.' *Harvard Business Review* (May–June 1985): 73–84.

Rahim, Syed A. 'Diffusion Research – Past, Present, and Future.' In Schramm and Lerner, pp 223–225.

Rhoades, Robert E. 'Tecnicista Versus Campesinista: Praxis and Theory of Farmer Involvement in Agricultural Research.' In Matlon *et al*, pp 139–150.

Richards, Paul. 'Community Environmental Knowledge in African Rural Development.' *IDS Bulletin* 10:2 (January 1979): 28–36.

Richards, Paul. *Indigenous Agricultural Revolution: Ecology and Food Production in West Africa*. London: Hutchinson & Co. (Publishers) Ltd, 1985.

Rouche, Laurence. 'Major Trends and Issues in Forestry Education in Africa; a View from Ibadan.' *Commonwealth Forestry Review* 54:2 (1975): 166–175.

Rogers, Everett M, and Shoemaker, F Floyd. *Communication of Innovations: A Cross-Cultural Approach*. New York: The Free Press, 1971.

Rogers, Everett M. 'The Passing of the Dominant Paradigm – Reflections on Diffusion Research.' In Schramm and Lerner, eds, pp 49–52.

Rogers, Everett M. 'Where Are We in Understanding the Diffusion of Innovations.' In Schramm and Lerner, eds, pp 204–222.

Rosenberg, Nathan. *Inside the Black Box: Technology and Economics.* Cambridge: Cambridge University Press, 1982.

Rothwell, Roy, and Gardiner, Paul. 'Design and Competition in Engineering.' *Long Range Planning* 17:3 (June 1984): 78–91.

Rothwell, R, and Gardiner, P 'Invention, Innovation, Re-Innovation and the Role of the User: A Case Study of British Hovercraft Development.' *Technovation* 3:3 (August 1985): 167–186.

Rothwell, R; Freeman, C; Horsley, A; Jervis, V T P; Robertson, A B; and Townsend, J. 'SAPPHO Updated – Project SAPPHO Phase II.' *Research Policy* 3 (1974): 238–291.

Roy, Robin, and Wield, David, eds. *Product Design and Technological Innovation.* Milton Keynes: Open University Press, 1986.

Ruttan, Vernon W. 'Assistance to Expand Agricultural Production.' *World Development* 14:1 (January 1986): 39–63.

Sansom, Robert L. 'The Motor Pump: A Case Study of Innovation and Development.' *Oxford Economic Papers* (March 1969): 109–121.

Sarin, Madhu. 'Improved Wood-Stove Dissemination by Village Women: The Case of the 'Nada Chula'.' In Clarke, Robin, ed, pp 130–138.

Satti, Kamal Mohamed Osman, Dorré, Jon Marlowe. *Charcoal Conversion Efficiency in Sudan's Traditional Earth-Covered Kiln.* Khartoum: Forest Administration, FAO, National Council for Research, and USAID, August 1985.

Schatz, Sayre P. 'Economic Environment and Private Enterprise in West Africa.' In Teriba and Kayode, eds, pp 35–46.

Schearer, S Bruce. 'The Value of Focus-Group Research for Social Action Programs.' *Studies in Family Planning* 12:12 (December 1981): 407–408.

Schramm, Wilbur, and Lerner, Daniel. *Communication and Change: The Last Ten Years – and the Next.* Honolulu: The University Press of Hawaii, 1976.

Schumacher, E F. *Small Is Beautiful: A Study of Economics as if People Mattered.* London: Blond & Briggs Ltd., 1973.

Scoble, G P W. 'Marketing Strategy Guidelines for Wood Stoves.' In Clarke, ed, pp 50–58.

Shah, S A. 'Growing Wisely or Growing Well? The Case for Eucalyptus.' *Indian Express* 15 July 1984, Express Magazine, pp 1, 6.

Shanklin, W L, and Ryans, J K, Jr. 'Organizing for High-Tech Marketing.' *Harvard Business Review* (November-December 1984): 164–171.

Shaw, Brian. 'The Role of the Interaction between the User and the Manufacturer in Medical Equipment Innovation.' *R & D Management* 15:4 (October 1985): 283–292.

Sid Ahmed, Khalafalla. *Seedling Demand for Khartoum Province.* Khartoum: Energy Research Council, March 1985.

Singer, H. *Report to the Government of Indonesia on Improvement of*

*Fuelwood Cooking Stoves and Economy in Fuel Consumption.* FAO Report No. 1315. Rome: FAO, 1961.

Skutsch, Margaret McCall. *Why People Don't Plant Trees: The Socio-economic Impacts of Existing Woodfuel Programs: Village Case Studies, Tanzania.* Discussion Paper D–73P, Energy in Developing Countries Series. Washington, DC: Resources for the Future, March 1983.

Smith, Adam. *An Inquiry into the Nature and Causes of the Wealth of Nations.* Edited by Edwin Cannon (from the 5th edition). Chicago: University of Chicago Press, 1976.

Soumare, Moustafa. 'Improved Stoves in Mali.' In Clarke, Robin, ed, pp 182–190.

Steel, William F. *Small-Scale Employment and Production in Developing Countries: Evidence from Ghana.* Praeger Special Studies in International Economics and Development. New York: Praeger Publishers, 1977.

Stewart, Frances, and James, Jeffrey. *The Economics of New Technology in Developing Countries.* London: Frances Pinter (Publishers), 1982.

Sudan Renewable Energy Project. Charcoal Production Implementation Plan. Khartoum: December 1983.

Sudan Renewable Energy Project. *Second Annual Work Plan: July 1984 – June 1985.* Khartoum: Energy Research Council, 31 May 1984.

Sudan Renewable Energy Project. *Third Annual Work Plan [July 1985 – June 1986].* Khartoum: Energy Research Council, May 1985.

*Sudjarwo, Aryanto. 'Yayasan Dian Desa's Wood-Conserving Stoves Project.' In Clarke, Robin, ed, pp 158–166.*

*SUNA (Sudan News Agency). 'Seven Killed in Shooting.' Sudan News Agency Daily Bulletin*, Issue No. 5308, 4 August 1985, p 8.

Suyono, Haryono; Piet, Nancy; Stirling, Farquhar; and Ross, John. 'Family Planning Attitudes in Urban Indonesia: Findings from Focus Group Research.' *Studies in Family Planning* 12:12 (December 1981): 433–442.

Tapp, Charles [CARE-Sudan]. Grant Proposal for the Expansion of North Kordofan Fuel Efficient Stoves Project. Khartoum: CARE-Sudan, 6 May 1985.

Tapp, Charles W N. *Review of Forestry Projects in Sudan.* Khartoum: Agricultural Research Council and USAID, September 1984.

Teriba, O, and Kayode, M O, eds. *Industrial Development in Nigeria: Patterns, Problems, and Prospects.* Ibadan: Ibadan University Press. 1977.

Tokman, Victor E. 'An Exploration into the Nature of Informal-Formal Sector Relationships.' *World Development* 6:9/10 (September–October 1978): 1065–1076.

Tyndall, Brad. 'Agroforestry: A Shady Deal.' *Sudanow* (July 1985): 42.

Tyndall, Brad. Report: Tree Nursery Workshop, February 15 – February 22 1985. Khartoum: March 1985.

United Nations. *Proceedings of the United Nations Conference on New Sources of Energy: Solar Energy, Wind Power, and Geothermal Energy,*

21–31 August 1961. UN Document No. E/Conf. 35/6. New York: United Nations, 1964.

United Nations, Educational, Scientific, and Cultural Organization. *Statistical Yearbook, 1985*. Paris: UNESCO, 1985.

US Agency for International Development. *(Draft) Africa Bureau Energy Strategy, 22 June 1983*. Mimeo, transmitted to Sudan Renewable Energy Project by memorandum from USAID Sudan Energy Advisor, 30 June 1983.

US Agency for International Development. *Evaluation of the Sudan Renewable Energy Project (Annex 2 to the Project Evaluation Summary (PES)*. Washington, DC: USAID, September 1984.

US Agency for International Development. *Rural Renewable Energy Project: Contract Number 650–0041–C–00–2002*. Washington, DC: USAID, 19 October 1982.

US Agency for International Development, Bureau for Africa. *Renewable Energy Technologies in Africa: An Assessment of Field Experience and Future Directions*. Washington, DC: USAID, April 1984.

US Agency for International Development, Bureau for Africa. *Report of Workshop on Forestry Program Evaluation, Lome, Togo, 7–11 May 1984*. Washington, DC: USAID, August 1984.

US Agency for International Development, Bureau for Asia. *Renewable Energy Systems Installed in Asia: Current Successes and the Potential for Future Widespread Dissemination*. Washington, DC: USAID, 12 April 1985.

US Agency for International Development and Government of Sudan. *Project Grant Agreement: Rural Renewable Energy Project, No. 650–0041*. Khartoum: USAID/GOS, 31 August 1981.

US Agency for International Development, The Inspector General. *Audit of ID Renewable Energy Projects*. Audit Report No. 9–000–86–3. Washington, DC: Regional Inspector General for Audit, 21 February 1986.

US General Accounting Office. 'AID's Renewable Energy Projects.' Mimeo, enclosure no. 1 to letter from Frank C Conahan, Director, GAO, to M Peter McPherson, Administrator, AID, 13 August 1982.

Volunteers in Technical Assistance. *Testing the Efficiency of Wood-Burning Cookstoves: Provisional International Standards*. Arlington, VA: VITA, 1983.

Von Hippel, Eric. 'Get New Products from Customers.' *Harvard Business Review* (March–April 1982): 117–122.

Von Hippel, Eric. 'User, Manufacturer, and Supplier Innovation: An Analysis of the Functional Sources of Innovation.' Draft, Sloan School of Management, Cambridge, MA, 1985.

Von Hippel, Eric A. 'Users as Innovators.' *Technology Review* 80:3 (January 1978): 30–39.

Weber, Fred. 'Technical Update on Forestry Efforts in Africa.' in USAID Bureau for Africa, *Report of Workshop on Forestry Program Evaluation*, Appendix B.

Whitcombe, Richard, and Carr, Marilyn. *Appropriate Technology Institutions: A Review.* The ITDG Occasional Papers Series, No. 7. London: Intermediate Technology Publications, 1982.

World Bank. *Gujarat Community Forestry Project Mid-Term Review Mission Report.* Washington, DC: World Bank, 26 January 1983.

World Bank. 'Land Tenure Systems and Social Implications of Forestry Development Programs.' Staff Working Paper No. 452. Washington, DC: World Bank, 1981.

World Bank. *Renewable Energy Resources in the Developing Countries.* Washington, DC: World Bank, January 1981.

World Bank. 'Sociological Aspects of Forestry Project Design.' AGR Technical Note No. 3. Washington, DC: World Bank, November 1980.

World Bank. *Sudan: Issues and Options in the Energy Sector.* Washington, DC: World Bank, 1983.

World Health Organization and United Nations Children's Fund. *Primary Health Care: Report of the International Conference on Primary Health Care, Alma-Ata, USSR, 6–12 September 1978.* Geneva: World Health Organization, 1978.

Yassin, Muna Ahmed. *The Nature of Land Laws in Sudan (With Specific Reference to Forestry).* Khartoum: National Energy Administration, April 1983.